# WHAT OTHERS ARE SAYING ABOUT RIGHT CLICK

*The cry of every parent and church leader in this generation is "How do I help create media-safe homes?"* Right Click *is a wonderful resource that gives practical answers to the most-often asked questions about how to handle social media. I loved the sections on setting limits and the importance of dealing with bullying and porn. This is my go-to book for parents.*

**— Dr. Jim Burns,** President, HomeWord, author of *Confident Parenting*

*As parents of two teenage boys,* Right Click *couldn't be more timely or relevant for us. We're so glad to discover it. This highly accessible book is not only grounded in research, it's immeasurably practical. If you're a parent, you'll want to read this book—and you'll be a better parent because of it!*

**—Drs. Les & Leslie Parrott,** authors of *Saving Your Marriage Before It Starts*

*My favorite thing about this book is that it doesn't take a doom-and-gloom approach to technology. It recognizes the bad parts AND the good parts, providing a road map for the future.*

**—Jon Acuff,** New York Times Bestselling author of *Do Over*

*As a parent of teenagers, this is the book I wish I'd had ten years ago before smartphones and social media challenged the skillsets of parenting. The first wave of trials and triumphs have come to pass, and* Right Click *captures the best wisdom and research to help future parents stand on the shoulders of those who have come before. Steal their wisdom and read this book; you'll be glad you did.*

**—Mark Matlock,** Executive Director, Youth Specialties, author of *Real World Parents*


*As parents, we find ourselves living on the "digital frontier." Like the pioneers who crossed the country to settle the Wild West, every step we take into this new technological landscape moves us further and further into uncharted territory. Figuring out how best to navigate the journey for our kids and for ourselves is not an option for parents; it's a necessity.* Right Click *will serve you as a wise and valuable tool in your digital parenting toolbox.*

**—Dr. Walt Mueller,** President, Center for Parent/Youth Understanding, author of *Understanding Today's Youth Culture*


*This is one of the first books I've read about technology that didn't make me feel defeated as a parent. Filled with practical suggestions and rooted in research, the FYI team avoids the typical approaches that vilify or glamorize digital connections. Raising culturally intelligent kids requires this kind of redemptive approach to technology.*

**—Dr. David Livermore,** cultural intelligence and global leadership expert and author


*Wise, practical, and fun to read. Parents will be delighted. And so will their kids.*

**—Dr. Quentin Schultze,** author, Center for Servant Leadership Communication

FULLER YOUTH INSTITUTE

*Right Click*
*Parenting Your Teenager in a Digital Media World*

A Sticky Faith Guide

Published in the United States of America by

Fuller Youth Institute, 135 N. Oakland Ave., Pasadena, CA 91182
fulleryouthinstitute.org

ISBN 978-0-9914880-5-6

Cover and Interior Design: Macy Phenix Davis, Matthew Schuler
Fuller Youth Institute

Copy Editor: Dana Wilkerson
Printed in the United States of America

For every parent wondering how to navigate
the maze of technology with their family.
**We've been there. We are there.**
**Every day.**
Your willingness to ask the tough questions
inspires us to do the same.

# RIGHT CLICK

### A STICKY FAITH GUIDE

## PARENTING YOUR TEENAGER
## IN A DIGITAL MEDIA WORLD

KARA POWELL, ART BAMFORD, BRAD M GRIFFIN

Fuller Youth Institute | Pasadena, California

# TABLE OF CONTENTS

# LOGIN [PREFACE]

*Please help us figure this stuff out.*

Tears in his eyes, our friend Tim confirmed for us that this book had to be written. His own experiences as a parent and a ministry leader left him with more questions than answers, and more frustration than resolution. When we pitched the ideas we had been mulling over—the ones that have come to life in the pages ahead—Tim's emotional reaction cemented our resolve to help parents find a way forward.

Kara and Brad are both parents of teenagers, pre-teens, and elementary-aged kids. That means we're knee-deep in the same (and daily!) conversations you are with our own kids and with other parents about digital technology. In fact, through focus groups and interviews, we listened to a host of parents as we developed this resource. Their hopes, fears, and practical ideas for navigating media are woven into every chapter.

Art isn't a parent, but he has been tutoring us in technology and digital media as a researcher who studies media, the ways we use it in our culture, and the role it plays in teenagers' faith formation. By serving as a youth ministry volunteer, he also has been able to evaluate much of the research he's conducted or reviewed firsthand to see what resonates most. We are incredibly grateful for his work quarterbacking this project alongside us (and a lot of other fumbling parents just like us).

Throughout the book, when we refer to "I" or "my," we may be referring to any of the three of us. It felt simpler to use just one voice rather than keep explaining who was talking.

# WHAT IS THIS RESOURCE ABOUT?

Early on in this project, we reviewed a number of existing research and resources on parenting and digital media, hoping to find a few we could recommend. A lot of what we found were resources trying to shoehorn responses to digital technology into a mold that was cast for analog media several decades ago. (Don't worry, we'll explain what that means in chapter 1.)

But like it or not, **we can't remove *digital* from our kids like a stain and get them to think about media and use it like we do.** That's not the world they live in now, and it's not the one they're going to live in as adults.

A host of resources also exist that tell parents *what to do* about the latest digital media fad rather than *how to think* about digital media more comprehensively. Many of these resources are good, and they are useful in the moment. **But relying on this kind of approach can begin to feel like a game of Whack-a-Mole for parents as new challenges keep popping up and changing.** The mallet that perhaps once worked now feels clumsy and ineffective.

We also can't deny the fact that each of our kids is different. What works for our oldest when she's fifteen won't work for our youngest by the time he's fifteen. As parents, we get exhausted from tracking down new tools to try to understand the latest device or new app our kids are obsessing over.

Finally, **we want to talk about media more with our kids, but we aren't always sure how.** And our kids can't seem to articulate anything coherent—or in a language we understand. As we'll explore in the coming pages, it turns out that we are living in a transitional phase in history. This means we as parents can—and should—have totally new conversations with our kids. We want to help you better understand where your kids are coming from and muster up the courage to talk more about all of this. As St. Francis of Assisi has been paraphrased, *Let us seek first to understand, then to be understood.*[1]

**So we wrote this resource to help you think differently about digital media, talk more with your family about it, and be inspired by the ideas of other parents navigating these same waters day after day.** A day rarely goes by in our families when new questions and parenting decisions about technology don't pop up. This book is as much about our own sanity as it is about yours!

For more resources to help build Sticky Faith in your family, visit stickyfaith.org. Look for free online features and extras related to *Right Click* at rightclickbook.com!

The stakes for how your family handles technology may be higher than you realize. One of the highlights of our research on how families can build long-term faith—or what we call Sticky Faith—has been the power of warm family relationships. Research indicates that children who feel close and connected with their parents are more likely to adopt their parents' faith.[2] **Every page in this book is geared to strengthen your relationship with your children,** which in turn increases the odds that they will follow in your faith footsteps.

So if you're wondering ...

*How do I raise thoughtful wireless users in a "Hey, Siri" culture?*

*What do I do when my eleven-year-old begs to get on social media because "everybody else is already doing it"?*

*How can I keep my teenager from becoming an Internet "troll"?*

*Can someone just help me reclaim face-to-face conversation with my kid again?*

... or a host of other questions, hopefully this book will kickstart good dialogue. We end each chapter with questions and suggestions for how you can both *teach principles* and *implement new practices* in your family.

We're in this with you. Digital media isn't our friend or our enemy. It's just part of life now. Let's chart a new path together!

## THE DATA: -----------------------------

### HOW MUCH ARE TEENAGERS USING DIGITAL MEDIA?

It is still very difficult to determine what is considered "normal" or average behavior when it comes to how young people are using digital media, but we know parents wonder how their kids' usage compares to others. The following statistics are not foolproof. They are also not meant to be a measuring stick by which you evaluate your kids. Instead, national averages can help us see the "big picture" changes that are happening in the lives of young people all around us. According to the latest findings:[3]

- 92 percent of teenagers report going online at least once per day. 24 percent of teens confess going online "almost constantly."

- 71 percent of teenagers use more than one social media platform to keep in touch with friends.

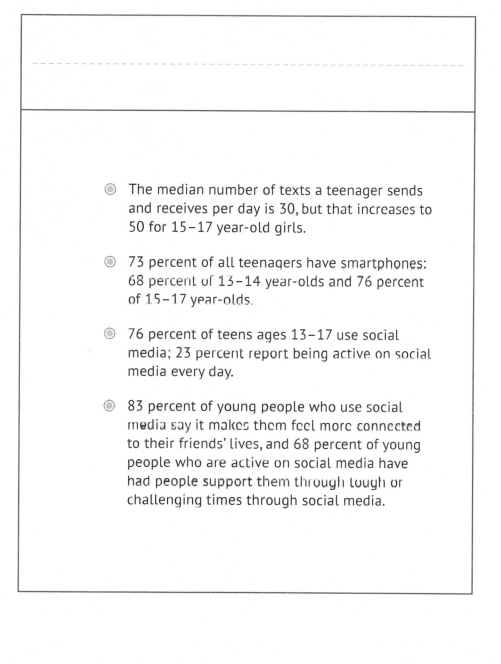

◉ The median number of texts a teenager sends and receives per day is 30, but that increases to 50 for 15–17 year-old girls.

◉ 73 percent of all teenagers have smartphones: 68 percent of 13–14 year-olds and 76 percent of 15–17 year-olds.

◉ 76 percent of teens ages 13–17 use social media; 23 percent report being active on social media every day.

◉ 83 percent of young people who use social media say it makes them feel more connected to their friends' lives, and 68 percent of young people who are active on social media have had people support them through tough or challenging times through social media.

# Ø1

## WHY RIGHT C‍L‍

# IT WAS EVERY PARENT'S NIGHTMARE COME TRUE.

"One afternoon the vice principal called me," Tammy said.[1] "He overheard a rumor that our son, Eric, had taken a photo of a particular body part with his phone and sent it to a girl in his class."

"I thought you might want to talk with him about it after school," the vice principal told this utterly mortified mom.

As you can imagine, Tammy's son emphatically denied sending the photo. They argued. Eric stood by his side of the story and accurately reminded his mom that he had never been in trouble at school before. But Tammy, who had always felt like she was close to Eric, knew she needed to dig deeper. She checked the statement from their service provider to see how many texts he had sent and compared that to how many were on his phone. Sure enough, she found that he had deleted several messages. After showing him this evidence, Eric finally admitted that he had, in fact, sent the picture.

Unfortunately his confession only led to another frustrating argument. In Eric's opinion, what he had done was "no big deal." Tammy decided to call a friend who works for the local police department to set up a meeting. "Eric either didn't get it or didn't care—I needed to do something more than just talk *at* him," she explained. Eric expected to sit through a quick lecture from their family friend at the precinct, but when they arrived, he was whisked into an interrogation room. A detective sternly explained the possible implications of sending these types of photos—which many states view as distribution of child pornography.

We asked Tammy, "So did he learn a lesson from that?"

"You bet he did. All three of our boys did."

Tammy handled the incident admirably. But most of us have *no idea* what we're supposed to do in situations like this. Kids have always made mistakes while they're growing up—that part is *normal*. But as Tammy bemoaned, **"This feels like a whole different level."** Mistakes like these can have very serious consequences, and as parents this is the water we swim in every day with our kids and their digital devices.

> *"I'D LIKE TO MEET THE GENIUS WHO THOUGHT, 'LET'S GIVE TEENAGE BOYS A CAMERA THEY CAN CARRY AROUND WITH THEM AND THEN GIVE THEM THE ABILITY TO SHARE PHOTOS ON A WHIM.' TALK ABOUT A COLOSSALLY BAD IDEA."*
> *—ANDRES, DAD OF TWO*

# IDENTIFY THE ISSUE

## WHAT DOES "RIGHT CLICK" MEAN?

*Technology is anything that was invented after you were born.*
—Alan Kay[2]

For several decades, with what feels like an ever-increasing momentum, our families have ushered one game-changing new system, appliance, or device after another into our homes—some into our kitchens, others into our garages.

But the ones that have caused parents some of the biggest headaches are those that land directly in kids' hands.[3]

We typically refer to a lot of our kids' technology as *media*. The origin of the word *media* essentially just means "middle."[4] And that fits, doesn't it? Media is intended to be an intermediary that connects people with one another, but often it ends up doing the opposite.[5] **It gets in the middle and drives a wedge between us instead.**

More recently, we've added new words to our media vocabulary: *social* and *digital*.

In both cases, these words differentiate our newer devices from the older *analog* ones we've been using for a while like radio, TV, film, and recorded music. Analog and digital may look and act pretty similar on the surface, but they actually have fundamentally different principles behind how they work (we'll spare you the details).[6] **The bottom line is that *analog* is a polite way of saying *old media*.**

When we say *digital media,* we're talking about a puzzle of computers, microchips, software, video games, and the Internet that coalesced together as one big phenomenon in the early 2000s.[7] Today this has grown to include laptops, smartphones, tablets, and any other interactive devices capable of connecting to the Internet. The two key distinctions that separate digital from analog are the ways in which digital media is *interactive* and *interconnected*.

What has been so tricky for parents about digital media is that **while it may look and feel a lot like the analog media we're used to, it's actually a whole new world.** The move to digital media is a way bigger paradigm shift than moving from cassette tapes to CDs, as radical as that felt a couple of decades ago.[8]

To use another analogy, we haven't just upgraded our baseball bat from wood to aluminum. We started playing hockey instead.

New paradigms require whole new perspectives to answer a whole new set of questions. But this is the rub: We only have old-perspective answers to new-perspective questions. This is why it can feel so disorienting. Scholars and experts used to be able to provide parents with straightforward and practical answers to their media questions. Parents had the sense that there were certain right and wrong parenting strategies when it came to media. Those waters are far murkier today.

Maybe you've felt this too. One mom we spoke with told us, "I'm so sick of the rules! We keep getting all this stuff from our kids' schools about what to do and it is usually *totally* unrealistic. It's no help." In fact, this year my kids' school sent home one newsletter encouraging us that kids shouldn't have more than an hour of screen time a day, and another newsletter saying they are supposed to spend at least an hour a day doing work on computer-based reading and math programs.

*What's a parent supposed to do?*

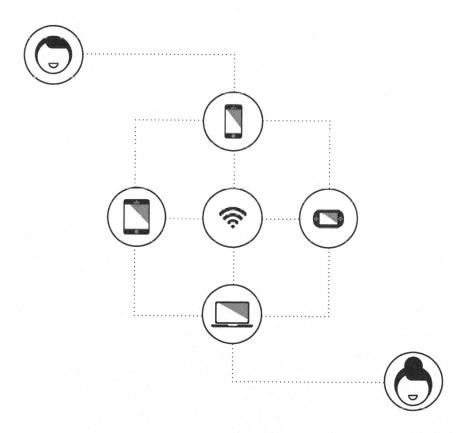

# NOT "**THE**" RIGHT CLICK, BUT **YOUR** RIGHT CLICK

When we talk about digital media in this book, *right click* does not mean a universally "correct" or "proper" way to click. **It's an invitation to step into the digital world of kids with greater understanding and create a plan that's right for your family.** When we "right click" on our devices, a menu appears that prompts us to choose what we want to do next. Throughout this book, we've sprinkled a host of options and suggestions, but ultimately you need to choose what fits your family best. We know families, but we don't know *your* family.

In the process of helping you devise a strategy that works for your family, we hope this resource helps you to step back, look at the big picture, and think about your options together. From this new perspective, you will hopefully find a handful of suggestions that alleviate some of your family's conflict or frustration over technology. If you have younger kids, you might even implement new ideas now that will help lay the groundwork for when they're older.

**More than anything else, our prayer is that technology will move from being something that drives your family apart to something that brings your family together.**

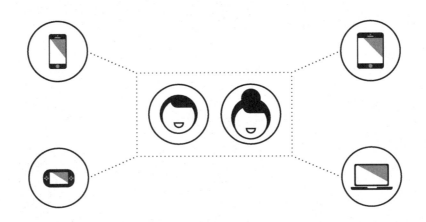

# REFRAME OUR VIEW

*SHIFTING MENTAL MODELS*

## ONCE UPON A TIME ...

Imagine a charming little village like the ones you see in fairy tales. It is part of a kingdom within which citizens travel and trade. Everyone speaks the same language, uses the same currency, marries within the same social circles, and holds the same values. Since the borders of the kingdom are well defined, its citizens enjoy both stability and peace.

Now imagine that one day the prince of this kingdom decides to marry a princess from a faraway land. At first, this is exciting news! People feel a thrill as they watch the people from this exotic new culture parade through their town on the way to the wedding. The royal couple even promises that this will be an era filled with all sorts of new opportunities that benefit citizens of both countries.

But after the honeymoon, the royal marriage slowly starts changing life across the kingdom—and life in our little village—even more than anticipated. The culture that has been treasured now has to adapt in order to accommodate new patterns of life. People start adopting practices from an unfamiliar new culture. A shift this monumental takes years, or even decades, before the dust finally settles.

*THE END.*

## PRETTY UNSATISFYING ENDING, HUH?

Well, this is where we live.[9]

Centuries ago, when one kingdom was conquered by or united with another, a long process of change would begin that touched on almost every aspect of people's lives. **We are currently in the midst of a similar shift as our existing world slowly adopts and adapts to its new partner in the wake of the digital revolution.** We remember how things were and the excitement of the wedding day (Remember your first smartphone?). But now we find ourselves caught in a world changing more rapidly than we imagined possible. The majority of marriages that end in divorce do so between the third and tenth year—that's where we are with digital media. There are good days and bad days. We're not sure how well this is really going to work out.

This presents us with quite a different set of challenges from those faced by our own parents and grandparents. The earlier transitions from print to radio, or from radio to television, were significant and had implications for how parents raised their kids. But these were all steps along the same path. Ours is a unique challenge because digital media has not simply taken the next step forward; it has leapt onto totally new ground.

**It is helpful to stop and let this sink in.**

So often we worry how we're doing as parents when it comes to media and our kids, but we truly are trailblazers. **If it feels like you're making it up as you go along ... that's because you are!**

It is also valuable to point out that our kids didn't ask for this. They're trailblazers too, but they just want to grow up safely and happily. This is more of a burden than we realize. When one group of researchers asked kids about their experiences online, they mentioned things like:

"Propositions to meet from people I do not know."
—BOY, AGE TWELVE

"One time I was looking for a game and rude pictures came on the computer, people without clothes on."
—GIRL, AGE TEN

"Pop up things where you have to buy something."
—BOY, AGE TEN[10]

The digital world can be a scary and confusing place for kids. As adults, we have perspectives of a world both with and without digital media. Our kids may sense that we miss how things used to be, but they'll never understand why.

They're just trying to make sense of the only world they know.

# A TALE OF TWO PERSPECTIVES

Kids are learning to understand and use media in radically new ways. **The biggest stumbling block for parents is often not what we do, but how we think about media.** When we fail to understand how our kids think about it, our conversations about boundaries, rules, and good decisions get lost in translation.

# THE FAULT IN OUR STATS

Throughout this book, we are providing research-based benchmarks to help you think about when and how to allow kids to begin using certain digital media. It is important that we include a caveat here. Based on the existing research, it is difficult for us to make these recommendations for three reasons:

1. *DIGITAL MEDIA IS STILL RELATIVELY NEW.*

   It's changing rapidly enough that there isn't much solid research available yet. A few years ago, I heard a scholar present his recently completed Ph.D. dissertation at an academic conference. He had done a rather brilliant study ... on MySpace. Immediately after he finished, every hand in the room shot up, eager to ask the obvious question, "What about Facebook?!" Now the questions would reflect the multitude of social media platforms.

   The kind of "media effects" research that is used to support usage recommendations gets better and better as more scholars are able to weigh in, tinker with variables, and retest certain hypotheses in different contexts.[11]

2. *A LOT OF EXISTING RESEARCH TREATS MINORS, COLLEGE STUDENTS, OR PARENTS AND ADULTS AS SEPARATE CATEGORIES.*

   It doesn't look at families as a whole or trace any progression from one developmental stage to the next.[12] This means that we do not yet have a clear sense of how much of what young people are doing online is just a digital version of them acting like adolescents and how much reflects the start of behaviors they will carry with them into adulthood.

3. *THIS IS ESPECIALLY TRUE WHEN IT COMES TO RESEARCH ON SEX, SOCIAL MEDIA, AND YOUNG PEOPLE.*

Topics related to sex and young people are notoriously difficult to investigate.[13] Most researchers steer clear of projects involving young people's sexuality or sexual behaviors because of all the approvals, permissions, and paperwork involved. That's why most of what we see in popular media is based on informal online polls rather than actual empirical study.

Even in the limited amount of studies we do have, it is difficult to trust the data. Imagine your kids being interviewed by a random adult stranger about their sexual behaviors, identity, or attitudes. Do you think they would feel comfortable or answer honestly? Does a seventeen-year-old boy respond differently to questions about his sex life when talking with a young adult female interviewer versus an older male one? Totally! It is very difficult to account for how the various age- and gender-related dynamics in these studies skew the results.

People in our position, translating this type of research into resources, don't do parents any favors by reducing complex studies into deceivingly straightforward statistics. We advise parents to take what they see in the news or hear about from others with a grain of salt and make sure they pay close attention to their own families.

We spoke about this with parents, and one mom, the wife of a research scientist, summed it up quite nicely: **"We don't worry about all that. They've done studies on kids, but they haven't done a study on *our* kids."**

# NAME THE GOAL

## *RELATIONSHIPS, NOT JUST RULES*

Having a big-picture grasp of what makes digital technology so different from what's come before helps us as parents to be equipped to deal with the questions and concerns we have now *and* be able to address future issues as they arise.[14] **The goal is to have great relationships with our kids. Media will be in the middle of that somehow.** Rather than a divider, we want it to be a middle ground—a *common ground* where families connect.

One dad we spoke with made a helpful observation about his own video gaming habits. Nicolas said, "It's funny because I always assumed I would outgrow video games at a certain point. I guess I thought that because my dad and my grandfathers never played them. But now I still love them and so do the kids, and that has been a big connection for us. We get to do it together." Nicolas noticed how, alongside the challenges we face as trailblazers, we also have a lot of great new opportunities to connect with our kids.

Megan, a mom from Michigan, actually thanked me at the end of our interview for a chance to pause and think about this. "You know, we've been struggling a lot lately, and I forget sometimes how we do enjoy technology together and even benefit from it. I'm grateful for that. I get frustrated at times, but at the end of the day, am I glad we have this stuff? Definitely."

"I was struggling recently with some things, and my nineteen year-old sent me a lot of encouragements by text. I thought, 'Wow, this has come full circle. I'm getting fed back spiritually now.' I try to tell parents that, because I think it's encouraging to know that it does come full circle." *—AMY, MOM OF THREE*

# RIGHT CLICK

## *COVENANT RELATIONSHIPS*

Many families, including our own, have found common media ground through covenant agreements. A covenant or "media contract" gives your family an opportunity to craft some language that describes how all of you will—and will not—use media. It helps create a consistent, shared way of life together— one in which everyone feels heard, valued, and where boundaries exist to connect us, not separate. Through the course of this book, we hope to help you create a covenant that is tailor-made for your unique family—your own "common media ground."

If an actual written covenant doesn't seem like a good fit for your family, that's totally fine. One mom of now college-aged kids told us, "We didn't do a written covenant, but I do think we had a kind of verbal covenant and consensus about what our expectations were." **That is the goal here: consistent consensus about your family's expectations.** In many cases, our prompts center around phrases like "Ask your kids …" and "Think about how …" Intentional reflection and conversation about media can itself provide a valuable "restart" for our current practices.

At points we will also suggest some changes in how we parents live out our own media use. That's the hard medicine to swallow here. As different as digital media is, our kids still observe and imitate how we use it. One of the things we learned through our Sticky Faith research is applicable to media: **You tend to get what you are.**[15] What we mean is that *our* faith is often the best predictor of our kids' faith. When it comes to digital media, we can safely assume that a similar principle is at work.[16] But our modeling is often unspoken, evolving, and involves our everyday lives and work.

# IT TAKES A NETWORK

When we sat down with parents in focus groups expecting to get some great questions and practical ideas, we often found that simply having a discussion about digital media was extremely helpful for parents. It provided an opportunity to share tips and strategies, many of which ended up in this book. Several of these church-based parent groups also realized that their kids were part of tightly connected social networks online, but they as parents were not.

With analog media, families only felt responsible for the media decisions made in their own homes. In one sense, it was an age of "every family for themselves." **Digital media has connected us to other families locally and globally in ways we've never before imagined.** That also means new doors have opened for parents to support each other more than we may realize. The more tightly knit and well connected your family's social network is both on and offline, the easier it will be to deal with digital media. We heard this theme in our conversations with parents. So as you read this book and think about the implications for your own family, consider expanding these conversations to include others, or even think about using this resource as a group study guide.

At the end of each chapter, we have included discussion questions to help us think together about digital media. You can use these with your spouse, friends, a book club, a small group, or your family. Our hope is that we can be more open and honest with each other about what we're struggling with in the midst of our changing world.

# "I THINK I FAILED AS A PARENT. TOTALLY."

Tammy was willing to share her story with us, and with other parents at church, even though it was an embarrassing "total fail" moment for her as a mom. She was comfortable admitting that when it comes to digital media, "I fail at it every time, but I have to keep trying. A lot of parents just look the other way, but I don't want to do that."

*We are all struggling with feelings of failure and fatigue when it comes to the constant challenges we face because of digital media.*

As we spoke with parents, we were struck by how negatively so many of them evaluated their own performance. These were folks who were recommended to us by their pastors and peers at church. And based on our research, we knew that many of these parents were all-stars. Yet in their own minds, they often thought the opposite was true.

So if nothing else, we hope you will be *encouraged* as you keep reading. You're probably already doing a much better job than you think! **Investing your time in reading this book is evidence that you refuse to parent in autopilot mode, and that's half the battle when it comes to digital media.** Let's get to work on this together! Our kids need us in this part of their world more than ever.

# DISCUSSION QUESTIONS

 1 When you hear the terms "social media" and "digital technology," what are the first few words, feelings, or thoughts that come to mind?

2 Imagine a typical day in the life of your family when it comes to using media. If we were flies on the wall at your house, who would we see using which devices, in what parts of the house, at which times during the day?
*TIP: Ask your kids this question—they might surprise you with their answers.*

3 At this point, what are your family's biggest struggles or tensions when it comes to technology?

4   How do you feel about your responses to these three questions? With whom else do you need to share those reactions?

5   Make a list of several ways you think your family's life is *better* because of digital media. What are some positives that you can celebrate and be grateful for?

6   If you are married, do you feel like you and your spouse are on the same page when it comes to digital technology? Why or why not?

# 02

# WHY DO MY KIDS CONSTANTLY CHECK THEIR PHONES?

# PUT THAT THING DOWN!

This was Betsy's first response when we asked a group of moms, "What comes to mind when you hear the phrase 'social media'?" The room burst out in laughter. Another mom chimed in, "That should be the title of your book right there: Put that thing down!"

The amount of time young people spend using digital devices seems to be one of the most pressing challenges for parents today. It feels like our kids are tethered to their phones, constantly glancing or full-on staring into a screen.

Before we judge our kids or insist they "put that thing down," we need to understand both what motivates kids to keep checking their devices and what we should do about it.

## IDENTIFY THE ISSUE

### THEY ARE DIGITAL NATIVES

It might seem pretty obvious, but the big difference between *media* and *social media* is the "social" part. Digital media was created and designed to facilitate better, faster collaboration and interaction.[1] So naturally, the ways we use digital media are inherently more social and interactive than types of analog media that preceded it.

But analog media is what we grew up with. **Researchers refer to today's adults as "digital immigrants," whereas our kids are "digital natives."**[2] Like most immigrants, we bring luggage from our pre-digital world, namely some of the expectations we have about why and how people use media. My grandfather moved to the United States from England when he was just four years old, yet he continued to have a hint of an accent from his native country (and a cup of tea every afternoon) until the day he died. In a similar way, we may use digital technology ourselves and feel like it is now "home" in some ways. But in reality, we will never be as fully steeped in digital culture as our kids.

Here's what that means: When we talked about media in the past, we presupposed a fairly passive type of engagement in which people would simply receive words, images, and sounds. Media was only *social* insofar as we could watch and discuss certain shows or movies together, sing along with our favorite music, or sit and read together. But now, it's a whole new world, and a social world at that.

"*I'LL SHARE SOMETHING ONLINE* and my kids will say, 'That's so '70s, Mom!' as if to say I'm posting like people did in the 1970s. Part of me wants to tell them we didn't even have computers back then, but then I realize that would make me seem even more ancient than I do now." —Melinda, mom of two

# WHAT ABOUT SCREEN TIME?

We used to be able to say with some degree of certainty that there was a threshold of "screen time" beyond which any young person's enjoyment would become detrimental to their health and development.[3] These negative effects were because of the inactive and often antisocial nature of being a media consumer. What kids were *not* doing while they watched—exercising, playing, studying—were (and sometimes still are) the problem. So our parents could say, **"Stop watching that or it'll rot your brain,"** and have some credibility behind their nagging. For the past several generations, parents have been setting time-based restrictions on listening to the radio or records, watching TV, talking on the phone, and watching movies.

This is why we instinctually feel like screen time is a bad thing that needs to be limited. Our parents set those types of limits for us, and now as adults we're probably really grateful they did. Today's parents expect that we too should be able to put those same sorts of straightforward numerical caps on our kids' screen time and media use because, for as long as anyone can remember, that's what parents did! And for younger kids, this can be a pretty useful strategy.

But for teenagers, times have changed. **"Screen time" is a bit too oversimplified to describe how young people use digital technology.** On the one hand, there are still some teens who mindlessly, antisocially surf, scroll, and stare at a screen for hours on end, not unlike the so-called "Vidiots" who were glued to cable TV in the 1980s.[4] But a majority of kids today use digital media in far more interactive and meaningful ways than we may realize.

Rather than "screen time," we might talk about "screen investment." It's no longer simply passive, but a multisensory engagement.

As adults, we have adjusted the way we use media to adapt to the social nature of digital technology, but our kids have never known a world where media meant *not* participating. We view digital media as more interactive than when we were younger. Our kids lack that point of comparison. **In their world, media *means* interactive.**

An important first step for us as parents is to recognize that we have to break the mold when it comes to how we parent in a digital world. **Screen time limits are definitely still helpful,** but we need to think more thoroughly about how and why we set these boundaries as kids get older. All-night marathon gaming sessions? Taking the phone to bed? Texting at dinner? Talking about boundaries is a must. But because media means something different to our kids than it did to us as kids (or even to us now), our responses need to be more thoughtful and nuanced than we might expect.

# ASKING THE REAL
# *WHY* QUESTION

So why *do* our kids constantly check their phones and other devices? Media researchers help us answer this question by distinguishing between "uses" and "gratifications."[5]

This is a bit like diagnosing the cause of an illness rather than just addressing the symptoms. For example, depression can cause many people to feel sluggish and tired. Drinking a cup of coffee might alleviate those symptoms a bit, but you can't say coffee effectively treats clinical depression. So just like medical researchers are primarily interested in the causes of an illness, media scholars don't simply observe *how* people use media but also unearth *why* they use it.

Let's say I asked you about your favorite TV show and why you enjoy it. You might tell me, "It's funny and full of great

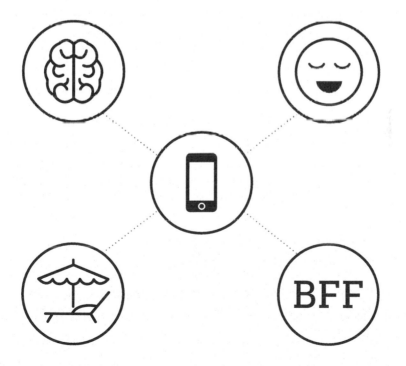

## HOW YOUNG IS TOO YOUNG?

If you're like us, you have wondered more than once what age is the "right" age to start using a particular digital device, app, or social media platform.

When we talk with parents about this, many express feeling like they're holding the line in a battle for as long as possible. They feel constant pressure, from multiple sources, for kids to start using more and more digital technology at earlier and earlier ages.

That cultural pressure makes this question particularly tough. We can tell you what doctors recommend, what legal regulations say, or various other pros and cons; but when your kids' school *tells you* they need an email account, or their coach *tells you* they will be coordinating practice times by text message, or **your teen comes home and *tells you* the irrefutable sad refrain, "*All* my friends have one!"**—the data seems to go out the window. Here are a few tips:

1. *LISTEN TO WHAT THE DOCTORS SAY.*
   The American Association of Pediatrics recommends keeping "screen-free zones" in the house, especially a young person's bedroom, as well as "screen-free times" like during meals. They also recommend just one to two hours of entertainment screen time per day and zero screen time at all for children under two years old.

   Keep in mind that these are the same people who recommend brushing your teeth three times a day, sleeping eight hours a night, daily exercise, and a well-balanced diet—they set the bar at "best-case scenario." But that best-case scenario is based on what's good for our bodies, minds, and emotions. Aiming high never hurts.

## 2. THE MAGIC NUMBER IS 13.

The minimum age required for Facebook, iTunes, Gmail, Pinterest, Snapchat, Instagram, and a host of other social networks is 13. If you have a child under the age of 13 who is using these platforms, you can appeal to terms of use and the current law (the *Children's Online Privacy Protection Act, or COPPA*) to draw a line.

## 3. TALK WITH OTHER PARENTS.

Most parents feel left on their own to make decisions about digital media. Agreeing to particular standards (like holding the age 13 lower limit) with other parents in your community provides some peace of mind and can be helpful when teachers, coaches, scout leaders, and so on try to push toward using particular contact platforms by providing strength in numbers.

## 4. REMEMBER WHY IT MATTERS.

These devices and platforms are to our kids like the Air Jordans, leather jackets, Walkmans, or whatever else were to you at their age. It is easy to get misdirected by questions of convenience, necessity, requirement for school, and so on. **What is at stake for a lot of young people when they ask, then beg, for these devices or networks is a feeling of fitting in and self-worth.** Take that into consideration, show empathy, and remember how important social access and status symbols seemed to you in your adolescent journey.

characters." But if I investigated further, I might find that your coworkers watch the same show, and you regularly discuss it together. So beyond simply enjoying the show, there is a social benefit—you feel more like part of a community in your office by sharing this interest. A lot of people might "use" media in the same way to watch the show, but viewers who talk about it with coworkers are gratifying a different need than those who just watch it alone.

As parents, we are often concerned with our kids' uses of media but unsure of their gratifications. When thinking about how our kids use media, it can be helpful for us to turn this equation around and first ask: **"What perceived needs or desires does this kind of use gratify?"**[6] By identifying these underlying motivations, we will be able to both understand our kids' media use as well as find outlets that meet these same needs through non-tech or low-tech activities.

"Claire used to love to read," a dad named Spencer told us, "but now she sits there on that phone all the time!" Spencer's concern is that the phone is replacing reading. But there's a different and deeper shift happening that Spencer might be missing. His daughter is getting to the age and developmental stage when connecting with friends often takes priority over more imaginative, self-focused play like reading. This new behavior may, of course, be partly about the phone, but it's probably mostly about social connection.

Maybe when Spencer was Claire's age, he fulfilled his social needs by talking on the phone (one with a curly cord that was mounted to a wall). **It's the same social motivation, but with a different technology to facilitate the hunger to connect.** If Spencer wants to provide opportunities for Claire to connect socially through different venues, one solution might be to organize a book club where Claire and her friends can split the difference. He might also encourage Claire to shift her interest from reading to writing as a form of self-expression by helping her set up a blog where she can share more focused and intentional posts with friends.

# REFRAME OUR VIEW

## SOCIAL MEDIA IS THE NEW SCHOOL LUNCHROOM

*IT IS ALWAYS DIFFICULT TO THINK AND REASON IN A NEW LANGUAGE.*

*—CHARLES BABBAGE[7]*

We've found it helpful to think about teenagers' use of digital media as today's version of the school lunchroom.

Teenagers have always seemed hypersocial to adults because they are in a stage of life when they begin to form their own identities. During adolescence, our brains tell us: "Okay, you're getting old enough to be your own person. So who are you?" Answering this question becomes a young person's number one priority. **The question "Who am I?" plays on a continuous loop, like background music in our subconscious, throughout adolescence.** Coming up with a sufficient answer to this question is a complicated and difficult job, and we work on it largely through relationships.

**School cafeterias have always been a kind of petri dish within which young people experiment with this "work" of identity formation.** The questions swirl around in a teenager's mind: *Where do I sit, and with whom? How are we dressed at my table compared to others? What do my peers do after school and on the weekend? How do we express ourselves and interact? How do we remember and talk about our good and bad experiences together?* These questions aren't usually this well articulated within the teen mind (much less out loud), but they're behind many of the behaviors endemic to lunchroom culture.[8]

To parents and educators, the noon break is about eating lunch. But for teens it can be the defining moment of the

43

entire day. It provides a space in which they can be themselves, but as people still learning who those "selves" are, it becomes a social laboratory. Every lunch is a kid's opportunity to experiment, tweak the formula a bit, and get ready to test out the new version tomorrow. The cafeteria experiment is filled not only with conversation, but also tons of non-verbal communication through students' seating location, clothing style, what and how they eat, and how they respond to each other.

In much the same way, being an active participant in social media is not limited to verbal interaction or one-on-one conversations.[9] **Parents often underappreciate how a quick scroll through social media for a teen can be like looking around the lunchroom.** Young people have very sophisticated ways of conveying social cues with digital media that we as adults struggle to recognize or grasp.

For example, I connected on a photo-sharing app with a student from my church. Within what seemed like a matter of seconds, he had liked every picture I've ever posted involving comic books. He breezed quickly through my few hundred other photos but stopped on these as if to say: "This is what we have in common; I like comics too."

Similarly, a young woman from our youth group chastised me one Sunday for never liking her social media posts. Her rationale for why I should like her posts was: "I *always* like yours!" Whereas I assumed that she genuinely enjoyed all my thoughtful, witty, and delightful contributions to the site (uh-huh, *sure*) she was actually just trying to figure out how the whole popularity game is played on social media. Regardless of what the contents of our posts were, she had affirmed my self-expression online and felt that I ought to do the same in return.

Many of these cues are non-verbal because young people still lack the capacity to express what they're thinking and feeling in words. These non-verbal messages also allow them to efficiently send

 (Want to go get pizza for dinner?)

(I can't. I have homework.)

 (Bummer! I wish you could go.)

the equivalent of a thousand words with one image. That's why phenomena like emoji and photo sharing catch on like wildfire (and continually evolve). This is also why **monitoring the "economy" of likes, shares, votes, and views is so incredibly important for young people**. And the irony of the lunchroom analogy is that often today's teenagers are also using digital social media in their *actual* school lunchrooms, navigating all these layers all at once.

*THOSE LAST FEW PARAGRAPHS CAN BE A GAME-CHANGER FOR UNDERSTANDING YOUR TEENAGER. GO BACK AND READ THEM AGAIN.*

Several decades ago, an anthropologist asked an indigenous native of a particular culture to explain the dance he had just seen performed. The native replied, "If I could tell you what it meant, there would be no point in dancing it."[10] That is roughly the dilemma our kids face, with an added buffer of immaturity. They know what they're doing feels very important, but they aren't mature enough to explain it or understand why. And it feels foolish to try to take the time to explain it to foreigners like us.

So to answer our question of what needs or desires our teens are seeking to gratify: Young people use digital media as a resource to help them define themselves and develop the social connections vital in adolescence.[11]

**Our assumption as digital immigrants is that screen time means being disengaged or antisocial, but when teens use social media, the opposite is often true.** As they perceive it, they're not just checking their phones—they're *checking in* with each other. They are sharing, scanning, and absorbing an onslaught of important social cues, even with a twenty-second glance at their handy device.

"We recently had eleven teenagers together for a weekend, and at one point while they were playing cards, four or five of them were on their phones. At first it was irritating, but then I realized that they were communicating with and including friends in the group who weren't able to be there physically. They weren't disengaging, but were actually increasing the social interaction beyond the group directly present. After a few minutes, all phones were down and everyone was engaged, and the friends who weren't there had been included in some small way. This is a whole new world." —JULIANA, MOM OF TWO

# NAME THE GOAL

*MORE CONNECTION. LESS GUILT.*

When adults check our phones, it's often relational (though many of us also use phones and other devices for work, which creates a complicated scenario we'll explore in chapter 3). We view texts, missed calls, emails, and perhaps social media platforms that keep us connected with friends and family (including our kids). But we're doing these things from a place of knowing who we are and how we fit in the world around us.

For our adolescent children, checking in is even more significant because our kids' identities are wet cement waiting to be influenced by the impressions of others. They are not passively staring at content, but are actively communicating with words, images, videos, and sounds.

To be clear, **we are *not* suggesting a free-for-all** where kids use their devices as often as they want. We will get to the issue of helping your kids learn to set limits and boundaries in the next chapter—don't worry! Our hope is that this chapter has helped you feel a bit less anxious about how often our kids seem digitally connected. For a lot of them, this can and will be a passing phase, not signs of a lifelong addiction.

Understanding the powerful social drives behind my own kids' texting has helped me relax at home. Our oldest two children are very close and have many mutual friends at church, so they often end up on the same group texts. That means that every time a group member sends a text, not one but TWO devices beep in our house.

I'll admit: It used to drive me crazy. I could feel my shoulders tense and my jaw tighten every time the chimes announced a new text—in stereo. Especially when it happened about every 20 seconds.

But then I remembered two realities: First, these are friendships that I hope grow. Second, when I was a teenager, my mom purchased an extended cord for our family room phone so that every afternoon I could drag it into my room to talk to my friends. Even though I had seen those friends that day, we still "needed" to talk about homework, relive what happened in P.E., and make plans for next weekend. Now my teenage children "need" those same kinds of connections, but they're just using different technology.

Another parent shared, "I think the natural reaction we have as parents is that we're being forgotten or replaced. It's like when we declare 'family day' because our kids are on the go with their friends. Family day or technology restrictions are often used because we feel we're losing connection, or even control. Truly understanding where our kids are coming from takes the parent vs. technology competition away and can provide new categories and less hard feelings."

In one of our focus groups, a mom named Sonia told us she had been similarly concerned about how much time her son spent glued to their tablet. When she investigated what he was doing, it turned out he and a friend were devouring and sharing information about tanks from World War II. One of their favorite video games had sparked an interest in learning more. She got him several books and videos about tanks, and they took a day trip together with his friend to a museum to see the real thing. In the process, Sonia showed her son how to take an online interest and transform it into a fun offline experience with a friend.

"I used to be really happy when we traveled to places with no Wi-Fi where the kids had no access to technology for a while. But once they had phones they could check in anywhere. On a recent international trip when we had no phone access, but did have Wi-Fi at the hotel, I noticed something different. When our kids had access to connecting with their friends, it allowed them to enjoy the experience of our travels all the more—because they could share it with their communities. Because they were unable to connect their phones while we were out and about, we had great connection without distraction. But then when we returned to the hotel, they could get online and make meaning of our experiences with their friends." —MARCOS, DAD OF TWO

# RIGHT CLICK

## BEYOND "TERMS OF USE": HOW TO START YOUR FAMILY COVENANT

As you think about creating some kind of family media covenant, make sure the question of "Why?" is also a priority. When your kids reach for their phones, is it because they want to "turn on, tune in, and drop out" as the 1960s counterculture mantra put it, or because they are biologically programmed to be hypersocial during this stage of life? If the latter is the case, **how can those needs be met in both digital and non-digital ways?**

A helpful way to start your family's covenant is a preamble or mission statement that defines why you use media and the benefits or value you hope to derive from it. Here are a few prompts to get you started:

- ◉ Explain the role you see media playing in your home. For example, "Media will be used as tools for building stronger relationships, learning, creating, and exploring interests and hobbies."

- ◉ Be intentional about wanting to *use* media for something (e.g., communicating, learning, family connection, even relaxation) as opposed to having media become a way of "doing nothing," and in the process *being used* by it. So your next sentence could be something like: "We set the following limits so that we will not become zombies who go through life glued to a screen."

- ◉ Affirm that, when used as tools, media can enrich our lives in significant ways. Project the positive outcome that will result when your family follows the rules and provisions in your covenant: "Media can be something that draws us closer together as a family, and we are grateful for that!"

Ultimately, we want to help our kids develop an awareness of why they feel an impulse to use media. This sense of awareness is what will allow them to make more thoughtful and intentional choices both now and as adults someday, no matter what context they're in or what new technologies come along.

Christine's sixteen-year-old son, Tyler, made an observation that she was proud to share with us. As his birthday party was wrapping up, Tyler said, "You know, Mom, I've been here for three hours and haven't checked my phone once." And it was true; he had been talking with his eighty-two year-old grandmother and having fun with extended family and friends the whole time.

But then he added, "All the adults have been on *their* phones the entire time, taking pictures and videos and everything. The adults are the ones who can't manage this stuff, not us." Christine concluded, "I think he was right. I think their generation is moving on. **Once they start getting a little older, they're being much better about this than we are.**"

If we as parents can get past our desire to toss our kids' phones out the car window when it feels like they aren't paying attention to us and remember *why* that last text feels to them like a social lifeline, Christine might just be right.

# DISCUSSION QUESTIONS

1   Think about your own use of digital or social media. What motivates you to check your texts, send that email, or poke around on social media? How is that similar to your teenagers' motivations to do the same? How is it different?

2   You might have started this chapter concerned about how much your kids are engaged in media or how many texts they send or receive per day. Does understanding *why* your kids are on their devices so much lessen any of those concerns? Why or why not?

3   How do you feel about your kids' connections in both digital and non-digital environments? Are those two ways of connecting balanced, or is one too dominant? If the ratio between digital and non-digital connection feels lopsided, how can you help your child find a more balanced approach to relating with others?

4   How do your answers to these questions differ between younger and older kids in your family? How might your approach need to be different with different kids?

# 03

# HOW CAN I HELP MY FAMILY ACTUALLY BE TOGETHER

## WHEN WE'RE IN THE SAME ROOM?

# AS A SEVEN-YEAR-OLD, THE CABIN FELT LIKE IT WAS IN THE MIDDLE OF NOWHERE.

And it probably was.

My brother and I charged into the vacation cabin our family had rented for the week, threw our stuff on our bunks, and started inspecting our new home away from home. We opened every cabinet and door, and then we slammed each shut.

"What are you looking for?" my grandpa calmly asked.

"Where's the TV?!?" we said with panicked looks on our faces.

"There is no TV," he answered. And get this: He seemed totally undisturbed by the idea of going a week without TV—*a week of vacation* even.

Our family stayed up that night playing a card game, and then we went outside to look at the stars. To this day, that week is one of my happiest childhood memories, despite the fact that I thought a TV-less cabin would doom us to endure the worst family vacation *ever*.

Today, there are few hotel rooms or vacation cabins that come without TVs. If your kids are like most, they're bummed when your family stays overnight someplace that doesn't have complimentary Wi-Fi (the nerve!).

When we are on vacation with our families, our various devices are like ocean currents that can cause us to drift apart from each other. **At home, the tidal wave of technology that pulls us in separate directions is usually even stronger.** In the midst of the challenges of finding tech-free shelter in an uber-tech world, the goal of this chapter is to help you create healthy media rituals and routines that fit your family and work with the ebbs and flows of your unique schedule.

"My fifteen-year-old son had a math tutor who was the mom of a toddler. Between her baby and his sports schedule, it was difficult to coordinate a regular time for them to meet. I came up with the idea that they try texting each other! For the entire year, they would text pictures and work out trigonometry. We set boundaries in the beginning: He could email or text any questions he had whenever he had them, but she would only respond during certain windows of time. It was the MOST amazing thing, and truly a gift for all of us involved. Plus, I didn't have to drive him anywhere."

—JANICE, MOM OF THREE

# IDENTIFY THE ISSUE

## THE BEST BOUNDARIES AND RIGHT RITUALS FOR YOUR FAMILY

In addition to being social, digital media is also unique because it is *mobile*. Unlike yesterday's portable Game Boys and Walkmans, *mobile* means that these devices stay on and stay connected constantly. In today's world, we have lost the ability to use the power-on-and-off switches for many of the devices we carry with us throughout the day (and, in fact, many of us rarely power off our devices overnight). As parents, we worry about the implications for our kids, as well as our relationships with them.

**We who are digital immigrants still have some sense of what researchers have called "media rituals."**[1] We remember when we could only access and use certain media in designated times and places: the TV in the family room, a radio in the car or bedroom, and a movie at the theater.

The nice thing about this ritualistic aspect of analog media was that it gave us a sense of togetherness. Even though family members might use media separately and in different rooms, the family had expectations about when and where we would use media. Nobody took the morning newspaper to their bedroom to read it at night or dragged the family TV set into the kitchen to watch pre-recorded late night talk shows during breakfast the next day. Of course, many of us still use broadcast media, whose content reflects what time of day it is: morning, daytime, evening, and late night, and adheres to time increments like thirty-minute programs and daily or weekly publication schedules. It has built-in time and place limits.

What many parents call "screen time" today is an attempt to establish that same kind of consistency and sense of routine with digital media. But once your child comes to own or access devices regularly, this is *extremely* difficult. We could limit screen time when it was just TV, a game system, or even a video on an iPad, **but once kids start texting, screen time becomes more diffuse and omnipresent.**

Digital media doesn't just lack that kind of stability; it often seems to go a step further and interrupt our daily rhythms and feeling of togetherness as families. So as parents raising digital natives, we need to reimagine what family time looks like and come to terms with the surprising ways that technology both helps and hinders our bonding.

# REFRAME OUR VIEW

## *PLAY TOGETHER, STAY TOGETHER*

Grown-ups tend to use digital media as a kind of hybrid of other media—we watch videos, read articles, listen to music, send email, and so on. We might *enjoy* doing these things, but enjoyment is not the same thing as *play*. When kids use digital media, the experience for them is often one of play. It might not look like we expect when we hear that word "play," but in their minds, they're making sense of it in much the same way.

Play can be solitary or social. It can be silly or serious. It can be goal-oriented or for its own sake. What is unique about play is the self-directed, spontaneous nature of it.

When we're doing something and aren't entirely sure what the outcome will be, and it produces that exciting, enjoyable kind of uncertainty, that's play.

*If we could experience digital media through our kids' eyes, it would look a lot like a playground.*

What we have learned to see as a jungle gym here and a swing set there, kids see as infinite opportunities for play. They might run laps around the swing set or climb up the side of it rather than swinging. The jungle gym's bars, platforms, and slides can be instantly transformed into a pirate ship, a magic castle, or a space shuttle.

This is why, even at an early age when outdoor and non-tech play continues to be vitally important, kids are so drawn into digital media. Their young minds experience the interactive nature and its seemingly infinite possibilities a lot like a playground, even through adolescence. What teens vaguely describe as "messing around" or "hanging out" is in many ways just their slightly more grown-up version of playtime.[2]

The rate at which technology has steadily evolved and improved in recent years has only served to amplify this even more. **What we see on our devices as new features and upgrades, our kids experience as new pieces of equipment on their playground.**

The way teens seem to migrate from one new app or game to the next every few weeks or months reflects their quest for play. Once the feeling of play wears off, they get bored and migrate to a new site. It is only as we get older that learning how to use something new starts to feel like a chore. For kids, it's a fresh slide to skid down (or even more creatively, to climb up). Eventually our kids will settle into using media in certain routine ways like we do as adults. But in the meantime, they are using digital media to collectively explore possibilities.

Plus, think about the messages that kids absorb about media.

**Kids live in a world filled with grown-ups who seem to be constantly checking or using their phones and laptops.**

Our current dilemma as parents is exacerbated by the fact that kids see the example of adults—including us—using our devices without knowing or understanding what we're actually doing with them. We might be doing work, posting on social media, or registering them for an upcoming church event. But they take the frequency of usage they observe everywhere they go as permission to go and use their own devices likewise.

"As a working parent, I'm often on my laptop around my kids, and I worry they feel like I work too much. But about one-third of the time, what I'm doing on my computer is for them. I'm emailing one of their friend's step-moms to set up a playdate, or I'm registering them for basketball camp. Whenever my time on my laptop is for my family, I narrate what I'm doing out loud so my kids can hear. 'Hey, Candace, I'm signing you up for piano lessons.' 'Zachary, I'm emailing Bennett's mom to invite him to come over next week.' I'm not sure if it means much to my kids, but it sure does lessen my guilt."

*—JOANN, MOM OF TWO*

In other words, "If Mom's on her phone, I can be on mine."

As families, we can begin by carving out specific spaces that are heavy-tech and low-tech. To this day I have never seen my mom talk with one of her friends on the phone in what we call our "family room." She might go take a call in the other room, but there is an unwritten rule in our home that the family room is just "us." In a similar way, if we want to make family time happen in our homes, we have to determine when and where it happens, and we must honor that as consistently as we can.

One mom we spoke with told us that something as simple as buying a new table had helped alleviate some of her media-related stress with her son. "We got this table that's in the family room for our youngest, and all his devices have to be on the table. That's where he has to use them." This simple change turned a lot of frustrated "no's" into clear expectations.

Similarly, while it is good to have screen-free areas around the house, it is helpful to clarify what those areas *are* for and explain our logic for why screens don't belong there. For example, we sleep in our bedrooms. Digital media disrupts our sleep in a whole variety of ways.[3] So it makes sense not to use or to have a media device in the bedroom. That is as logical as not taking your phone into the shower with you.

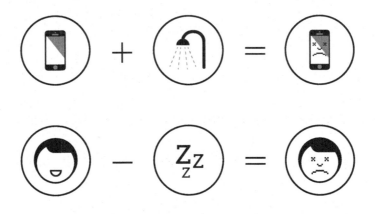

Screen-free zones are great for teaching kids boundaries, but we also need to connect the dots well enough so that kids understand *why* certain areas have the restrictions they do.

# NAME THE GOAL

## *MAKING MEDIA A PLUS*

"My son set up his whole video game system in our bedroom while I was recovering from surgery, hoping it would make me feel better. And he would sit there and play with me. It was so sweet."

*–MICHAELA, MOM OF TWO*

Parents often fail to meet kids in the middle when it comes to what quality time or "togetherness" means. As we discussed in the previous chapter, digital media is reshaping the nature of social interaction for young people today. When it comes to screen time, we want to help our kids develop *rituals*, or patterns of when, where, and with whom they use media.

**Researchers have found that when asked about their happiest memories involving family, a lot of kids describe times shared that somehow involved media.** This is *especially* true of new media, when young people got to be the family's resident expert and explain something to their parents for a change, rather than vice versa. Creative parents are diving into kids' technology as a way of entering their world. That means playing video games … and watching online videos … or getting better at text slang. We don't have to be great at it, and we'll probably embarrass ourselves in the process, but it is meaningful and endearing when we try.

"I have been summarily dismissed by my son that I do not know anything," Emily said, laughing. "And our daughters think it's funny because, well, I'm old. So I'll text them 'brb' or 'lol' or whatever and they laugh at me and go, 'Oh, Mom.'" Humility and a sense of humor like Emily's can go a long way. She also described working together with her kids on creative media projects. "We made a movie on my smartphone at one point, 'Favorite Memories of My Uncle,' which was really fun. We put together photos and video with some music and shared it with him."

In a similar way, recently our kids have started making movies together using a simple video app that quickly transforms short clips into epic movie trailers or short films. At first we weren't so sure they should be spending more time playing around with technology, but it's become one of their favorite things to do together. It is hard to argue with the level of creativity and camaraderie movie-making has sparked.

Our friend Adam McLane is a youth worker, web developer, and social media guru. We asked him about spaces and rituals in his own family (with a teenager, preteen, and preschooler) when it comes to technology, and he shared the following:

We have some household boundaries that we're quite rigid about. For instance, everyone in the house has to use Internet-connected devices in public spaces of the house. So you can't disappear into your bedroom with your tablet to play games behind closed doors. That also applies to Mom and Dad, who both work at home. We've made being online, playing games, watching videos, and working all fundamentally social activities.

That said, we don't have rigid time boundaries. In our house, we consider gaming or watching YouTube or what is commonly called "screen time" a free-time activity. On a typical school day, we have free time for an hour after school, then homework, dinner, and free time until bed. Many days, most of that free time is playing video games (or bouncing on the trampoline!).

My own bad habits have negatively impacted my kids' view of technology, though. A few years back I was taking my son, Paul, to a San Diego State football game. While we were on the trolley to the game, I realized I had forgotten my phone in the car. I said, "Paul, I'm super bummed I forgot my phone. Ugh!"

He looked at me and said, **"Dad, I'm glad you didn't bring your phone. Now you can be with me at the game instead of telling all your friends on Facebook you're at the football game with me."** Game. Set. Match. He was absolutely right, and we've had to be more aware that attention given to our phones is attention not given to them. When we went camping in Yosemite this summer, one of the best things I did was turn off my phone and lock it in the glove box. I didn't need it, and I would have fiddled with it instead of spending countless hours playing Bananagrams with my kids and their cousins.

# RIGHT CLICK

## *EVERYTHING IN ITS RIGHT PLACE*

As you create your family covenant, here are some categories to think about that might help you work to establish healthy media rituals:

———————————————————————— [o]

*WHERE:* Where do we use media together or separately throughout the house?

*WHEN:* When do we typically use media during the day and throughout the week?

*WHO:* Who do we use digital media with or without—family, friends, teammates, adults at church? What are appropriate ways to use media in those different relationships?

*WORK:* What times and places are devoted to work and to homework, and how are those distinct?

*PLAY:* When and where does play happen, and how is that uniquely set apart from work?

*RITUALS:* With these previous categories in mind, what might be a few consistent family rituals, with and without media, you can try to "carve in stone" on your family's calendar?

# PRACTICAL IDEAS

Some examples of rituals that are valuable to families we studied include:

- *One Family: One Screen* times, meaning everyone is watching the same screen (often a movie or playing video games together) without screen multitasking.

- Regular video chats with extended family members who live far away.

- Family game nights when members take turns choosing the game. Try mixing up tech and non-tech play. One dad likes to intersperse digital basketball with his kids with physical hoops before and after each video game.

- Sending positive, affirming text messages to each other (but for parents, trying to have a few consistent times that you do so as opposed to bombarding your kids with unwanted texts).

- Developing guidelines for when kids can use their devices in the car. Perhaps kids can't be on their phones as you're driving to school or on the first five minutes after you pick them up, since these are often golden times for family conversation.

- Encouraging your kids to look for apps that might resonate with what they are already passionate about. One family's daughter catalogued every book their family owned using a library app. It worked out well because she loved to read and was interested in working for a library someday.

# PRACTICAL IDEAS

- Digital scrapbooking or family archive projects (which can be great, tactile ways to think together with kids about family and media and let them be the experts).

- Designating a specific box, basket, or bowl to put devices in to avoid using them during certain times. One family keeps this in the center of their table during dinner, another by the door, and still another said they use it primarily when friends come over—more as a way of helping their kids' friends practice boundaries than their own kids.

- Setting up time restrictions to limit when or for how long kids' devices can connect to the family's Wi-Fi. Some parents made these open discussions; others were more covert. One dad, Carl, told us that he intentionally placed a second Wi-Fi router in a place that would interrupt the signal in kids' bedrooms. He explained, "You can't be too obvious about it, but I think making it even just a little inconvenient for them to download quickly and connect can be enough to nudge them away from overuse."[4]

- Treating going to a restaurant as a special occasion for the family to enjoy time *together*. Kids can only use their phones in "show and tell" mode, meaning they only use devices to pull up a photo or look up something everyone is talking about, not as an alternative to being part of the conversation.

- Inviting kids to do tech tutorials with parents and grandparents.

"I shared with them what the school sent home about Snapchat and how it was all about sexting, and they got to drive an honest conversation about it. In my family, tech tutorials have become a place where all of us feel safe to talk, share, teach, and in my case learn. I get to keep up with them because they're bringing me along!"

—TAMMY, MOM OF TWO

"The phones of our sixteen- and seventeen-year-olds need to be on their dressers or the dining room table at night. They can't be in bed with them. If phones make their way into bed, they end up in Mom and Dad's room to relieve temptation. That sleep is important."

—GAIL, MOM OF FOUR

# DISCUSSION QUESTIONS

 **1** How much does your family feel tension around digital media use in the home or car? What do you think are the causes of that tension?

**2** Imagine the floor plan of your home. What areas are for work or for play and relaxing? Where does your family seem to use mobile devices the most? How do you feel about that?

**3** Are there any certain times and places where you can establish new family rituals with and without media?

How can you involve your kids in helping establish these new rituals so that they have greater ownership in both the process and the end result?

 Based on the ideas that we've shared or that have occurred to you as you've read this chapter, what would you like to add to your family covenant?

# 04

## HOW CAN I SUPERVISE WHAT MY KIDS ARE SAYING AND SHARING

### WITHOUT MAKING THEM FEEL LIKE THEY'RE UNDER SURVEILLANCE?

## IN ADDITION TO **PUT THAT THING DOWN!** ANOTHER SUGGESTED TITLE FOR THIS BOOK WAS **HOW TO STALK YOUR KIDS ONLINE 101.**

This one came from Troy, a dad of four teens.

"I basically wish they had a stalking manual for parents," he laughed. "In a lot of ways it is all the same stupid stuff kids used to do behind your back, or in alleys or parks, but now they do it online. So it used to be the case that you would try to watch them, or could follow them and catch them doing stuff, like smoking at the park. Now you have to do that digitally ... somehow."

# IDENTIFY THE ISSUE

## IT'S A SCARY WORLD OUT THERE

"Mom, someone's been liking every photo I post and messaging me to say how much he loves my confidence. Now he wants me to send him more photos."

As Jeannie listened to her daughter, Emily, describe her new online friend, something seemed a bit off. But Emily's next sentence was the clincher.

"But I don't even know who he is. He's not from school or church, and my friends don't know him either."

At this point, alarm bells sounded in Jeannie's mind.

Jeannie explained to Emily how this could potentially be an adult man somewhere with not-so-good intentions. "Gross." That was all Emily said as she took her phone out and immediately began disconnecting from this stranger.

But as Jeannie pointed out to us in our interview, "If she hadn't talked with me about it and shown me what was going on, I wouldn't have known. That's why trust is so important—and the willingness to communicate."

As a responsible parent, you know you need to monitor your kids' media safety. But in today's digital world, it's no longer as simple as blocking certain cable channels or scanning labels on music. **You probably also wonder about the words, images, and information they are sharing online, via text, and through social media platforms.** The lines between all of these channels seem to crisscross and merge so quickly that we can't hope to keep up.

Trying to keep our kids safe in this traffic sometimes feels like walking ten steps behind a toddler as they wander across a busy freeway. It is very difficult to traverse the fine line between "stalking" our kids (as Troy put it) and keeping an eye on what they're doing, while also trying to build the type of trust that let Jeannie help Emily recognize a risky situation.

**Depending on how old your kids are now, your concerns about these issues probably differ.** Many young children will accidentally stumble across grown-up things (like crude humor, violent images, or pornography) that in most cases they would rather not have seen.[1] This kind of unwanted exposure can be unsettling, confusing, and even traumatizing. As kids navigate the teen years, curiosity adds to this mix as they both accidentally *and* intentionally engage adult content online, in video games, and through texting.[2] We want to keep our kids safe from porn, violence, bullying, and contact with adult strangers. But they naturally want to explore, and often they have access in more ways than we realize.

The good news is that we can help our kids learn how to stay safe and how to avoid, evade, and use best practices when facing these sorts of negative experiences with digital media—both when trouble is looking for our kids and when our kids go looking for trouble.

# REFRAME OUR VIEW

## *SUPERVISION, NOT SURVEILLANCE*

There's a big difference between *supervision* and *surveillance*. The way we use *surveillance* typically implies watching passively and waiting for any incidents that might warrant punishment. When we hear about surveillance, a lot of us probably think of cameras, wire taps, or guard towers that are used to catch guilty parties in the act.

When we say supervision, we usually imply that it's more personal. **Not something that watches over, but someone who pays attention to what I'm doing.** We don't supervise only to monitor boundaries and enforce rules. We supervise our kids to ensure that they play safely and nicely with their friends, and they can interact with us while they do.

As kids get older, they require less supervision. It is not just that parents trust kids to behave well; kids also need to trust themselves to know how to respond to whatever might come up *when adults aren't around.*

When it comes to the way we track with digital media, we want to help our kids learn how to:

1. Evaluate digital media sites and situations in which they're unsure of what to do or struggle to make a good decision.

2. Determine how to react as best they can (and quickly).

3. Have an honest conversation with us about their response afterward.

These three goals are best accomplished through two key family technology ingredients: trust and protocol.

# TRUST THEM

Because we are afraid our children are going to accidentally or intentionally view images online that we wish they wouldn't, **our tendency is to jump to restrictions as the first line of defense.** Restrictions are helpful in that they give kids a clear sense of what we expect from them. But sometimes kids encounter things online that *they* did not expect. They might be adhering to our restrictions just fine, but can still come across things that they know we would not want them to see. The restrictions we put on digital media can become a double-edged sword in these situations when kids expect to lose their device privileges or get in trouble for admitting to having had certain experiences. Thus they keep their online world secret from us for fear of the consequences.[3]

In addition, the anxiety we express in front of our children about online temptations can become a self-fulfilling prophecy. Researchers have found that in a number of situations the more *sure* parents seemed to be that kids were doing something bad, the more *likely* kids were to do it. **Treat kids as innocent until proven guilty, not the other way around.**[4]

As our kids learn media discernment and self-control, there will inevitably be some failures—maybe even painful ones. **Ultimately, what's as important as how many times our kids fail or succeed is how we respond to them in those moments.** As author danah boyd teaches, "Fear is not the solution; empathy is."[5]

One mom shared, "We trust them until they give us a reason not to. If there is a problem or issue, we talk them through it and then impose any additional safeguards or consequences we think necessary until they earn back the trust. We then give freedom back a bit at a time and build back trust. These are all teaching moments."

In an interview with the Fuller Youth Institute, boyd further explained, "When it comes to talking with [young people], the key is to get beyond the technology and get to the root of what's happening. It starts by neither fearing technology nor presuming it to be the center of everything. It's simply that which mirrors and magnifies everyday life."[6]

# TRUST YOURSELF

Using Troy's metaphor of following kids to the park to catch them smoking, we might consider *why* our parents did that. They weren't just aimlessly patrolling the neighborhood. They responded to things they noticed were different—an empty pack in the trash, a lighter in the sock drawer, or the smell of smoke on our clothes. Sometimes the newness of unfamiliar media distracts us in ways that cause us to miss these sorts of clues. The result can be a bit like driving around the park looking for our kids while they sit home alone.

In addition to trusting that kids are trying their best to meet our expectations, it is equally important that we trust our own instincts when it comes to whether or not something might be amiss.

"My son asked me to help him order something online recently, and as we walked through the process together, I was surprised about two things· I've become desensitized to the marketing on the margins of Amazon, and my son thought they all sounded like great deals that we had to click on! We talked in the moment about how click-marketing works, but he didn't seem to fully believe me."

*—ESTHER, MOM OF THREE*

# SET UP A PROTOCOL

In addition to open and honest conversations, it is important that we walk kids through what to do in unwanted and unsafe situations. We need to continually model safe media protocol, just like when we model looking both ways before crossing the street.

This could include making a habit of saying out loud what we're looking at or doing while using devices and describing how it makes us feel. "Oh wow, this website has gross photos. I'm closing it." Or "Look at this text. See how they're acting like they know me? I don't know them! A lot of messages like this are a scam—don't reply to them."

While these types of preventive conversations as well as various content filters, blockers, and rating systems can be helpful according to your family's needs (we say more about these at the end of this chapter), the unfortunate reality is that it's **not a matter of *if* our kids will encounter explicit content and unwanted interactions, but *when*.** Even as we try our best to uphold certain standards, we must also equip our kids with protocols for responding instantaneously to images we wish they never had to encounter.

Our kids need rehearsed ways of responding to and dealing with these experiences. Like other tricky areas of parenting, our silence about such matters teaches our kids to look elsewhere for help.

That means we role-play how to respond to toxic media situations just like we do with fire drills or "stranger danger." A few years ago, I asked my husband when he first encountered pornography; he was twelve and it was at Boy Scout Camp. Three years ago, our twelve-year-old son was headed to his own Boy Scout Camp. And thanks to digital options, children's first exposure to pornography is not getting any later.

So before that camp, we sat with Nathan and helped him think about how he could respond to pornography—both "old school" magazines and today's digital versions. We asked him to think about what he would say to someone who wanted him to check it out, and actually had him say the words aloud. (Yes, it is that fun being part of the Powell family).

As awkward as these conversations are at times, research indicates that they help.[7] One study found that "when parents do talk about pornography with adolescents, emerging adults' attitudes about pornography are significantly less positive. These negative attitudes, in turn, are associated with a reduction of emerging adults' pornography use.[8] What is important here is that these researchers didn't ask what parents actually said to their teens—it was as simple as, "Did your parents talk with you about it?" Those who answered "yes" viewed less porn as adults.

> "It's all about having open and honest conversation. We ask them what jokes their peers tell, what they have seen on apps, what their peers think about sex and porn, and where they think they need to be careful, and they will often give us what we need to guide conversations. We talk through where we are on these issues and discuss responses. Kids also need to be prepared for the second wave of response if they give their first practiced response and it's met with a challenge."
>
> —JODI, MOM OF TWO

# NAME THE GOAL

## *BUILDING INTEGRITY, ONLINE AND OFF*

When parents and kids make a habit of sharing what we're seeing and experiencing online, for safety's sake, we improve our communication and interaction with one another. When we invite kids to share the worlds they're exploring online, an overwhelming majority of what they'll share will be safe, fun places—like the playgrounds in our neighborhoods.

As we trust kids enough to have these open and honest conversations, we might be pleasantly surprised. **Most kids strongly dislike all the garbage polluting what, in their minds, should be a fun and safe virtual world.** Often they're trying to be kids and play by the ground rules their parents set for them.

The real problem here is typically not our kids. It's other adults. Advertisers prey on kids' attention. Pornographers abuse their natural curiosity. Kids who bully others mimic the abusive behaviors they see adults modeling all over the Internet. It is important that we don't blame our kids too severely for falling into these traps, set by grown-ups, that are difficult for all of us to avoid. It is truly an unfair environment for a young person to navigate alone. Which is why we recommend that you create an atmosphere in your home in which it's okay to talk about these struggles.

Your kids also need other safe adults in their lives with whom they can talk about some of these issues that might be really uncomfortable to discuss with you. So as you talk, identify together at least one adult they feel like they could talk to first when they aren't ready to talk to you.

Janie, a mom of five, pointed out how even our devices seem to contribute to the challenge. "I think it is just so isolating and getting increasingly more isolating. It's not something where you buddy up into the personal space of someone next to you and share whatever it is you're looking at with them. In general, they aren't making the screens bigger and more communal. Now there are watches and glasses that make the experience more personal, smaller, and more isolating."

**Perhaps a bit of good news is that every new type of media goes through awkward stages of growth very similar to the one we're in.** Kids and adults explore and push boundaries with new media, parents and society react, and eventually better systems of regulation emerge.[9] Media scholars, tech manufacturers, software developers, and policymakers are currently working to develop and implement better built-in protocols (for instance, websites with a .porn URL rather than .com) that eventually will help parents.[10] More and more schools are implementing anti-bullying programs that include digital bullying provisions as well. The project of cleaning up our online neighborhoods together is already underway!

One of the best things we can do in the meantime is **build bridges—rather than walls—between ourselves and our kids when they fail in these areas.** Well-known pastor Andy Stanley had a family rule when his children were teenagers: If they came to him and shared how they had blown it sexually, they would not be punished for their mistakes. If he found out from some other source, they would experience consequences. That was the only area in his and Sandra's parenting in which their kids had a "get out of jail free" card that exempted them from consequences. Some might find that extreme, but the Stanleys felt like their kids were better off being able to talk with them about their sexual struggles than keeping them secret for fear of parental punishment.[11]

## SEX & SOCIAL MEDIA

Our team spent a lot of time deliberating how to address topics related to sexuality and digital media, most notably pornography, which has become—and should be—a major concern for parents.

Ultimately, we decided not to devote a full chapter to porn and issues related to sexuality for two main reasons:

1. **The research on sex, social media, and young people leaves much to be desired.** See "The Fault in Our Stats" (Pages 26-27) for more on this. We will simply add here that in a lot of the material we reviewed, researchers expressed that they were skeptical about their own data because of various methodological challenges.[12] It felt irresponsible for us to share a work in progress with you as definitive data.

2. **This topic has as much to do with your teens' sexual development as it does digital media.**

   Many of the strategies throughout this book have proven to be effective in reducing the likelihood that a young person will view or share sexually explicit content. Boundaries, rituals, authenticity, and more open and honest conversations about how and why we use media will all help.

   That being said, we do not want to further perpetuate the idea that activities like sexting or viewing porn are just media problems. With sharing or viewing explicit content, parents often seem to want to focus on media as the problem in order to avoid having more challenging conversations about sexuality. As a result, young people turn to media *more* to address the questions and curiosity they have about relationships, sexuality, and romantic love.[13] Our role as parents involves helping kids to know what is appropriate and to learn to both moderate and express their sexuality in healthy ways as adults.

"I couldn't believe how well it went. Grace's boyfriend actually thanked us afterward for talking with him about it like an adult." Nikita told us about how she and her daughter had a face-to-face conversation with Grace's boyfriend (and his mom) after he sent her an inappropriate video. "They eventually broke up, and that was part of why, but I felt like I knew him and his mom better because of social media, which helped us to be able to talk. He and his mom both really appreciated it, and Grace learned that she can assert herself more in relationships, which is awesome."

Unfortunately, media brought some unwelcome images into Grace's life, but Nikita welcomed the springboard to dive into deeper conversational waters with Grace and her boyfriend. Nikita addressed the real issues in Grace's relationship rather than taking away her phone or trying to make her disconnect from her boyfriend.

# RIGHT CLICK

## STRATEGIES FOR FACING DOWN ONLINE DANGER

1.  *STICK TO THE BASICS.* Many of the basics we have described in previous chapters work in our favor here. Kids who have clear time and space boundaries and who regularly use and talk about media together with other family members are typically at a lower risk of succumbing to both the dangers and temptations they encounter online.[14]

2.  *TAKE SCREENSHOTS.* One of the biggest prevention protocols we encourage parents to learn and teach their kids is to take screenshots and send them to each other via private text messages. This can be something you do for fun as well as online safety—if one kid sends you something funny, screenshot it and share with the rest of the family.

    Once your kids know how to do this, encourage them to **quickly take and send you a screenshot of *anything* that makes them feel uncomfortable or confused.** This applies to both static content like photos on a site *and* social interactions they experience on apps, chats, and so on. You might also encourage them to share happy moments like the completion of a hard level in a game.

    When one of your kids sends you a screenshot of a negative interaction, send a reply confirming that you received it and discourage them from reacting or responding right away. Instead, encourage them to close or delete whatever it is and leave whatever site or app they're using, knowing that they can process it with you later. This teaches kids not to

## HERE ARE THE CURRENT COMMANDS
## FOR TAKING SCREENSHOTS:

**Mac:** "Command" + "Shift" + "3" saves a copy of your current screen to your desktop.

**PC:** The "PrtScn" key saves a copy of your current screen to your desktop.

**iOS (iPhone, iPad, iPod Touch):** Press "Home" + "Sleep/Wake" at the same time, and an image of your current screen will save to the Photos app.

**Android:** Hold "Volume Down" + "Power" for one or two seconds, and an image of your current screen will save to the "Screenshots" folder in the Gallery or Photos app.

respond impulsively or to continue exploring—both of which are impulse control responses that will be valuable as they get older.

Sharing screenshots can also work as great preventative medicine. Kids will recognize how digital content doesn't go away as easily as they suspect. They'll quickly figure out that others can capture what they are saying and sharing as fast as they can. As one mom we spoke with told us, "I grabbed my daughter's phone and took a screenshot of something on an app, which she thought would be instantly deleted, and texted it to myself. Then I showed her my phone and said, 'See? Now it's permanent. Oh and look, I can send this to all my friends, too.'"

3. *TRUST YOUR INSTINCTS.* In the next chapter we'll talk more about the research finding that kids' behavior tends to be very consistent on and offline. If your instincts as a parent tell you something is up with one of your kids, trust that and talk with him or her. As you do, remember that what's bothering them might not be something that happened in what we call "real life," but rather online. The line between on and offline is incredibly thin for our kids, and they interpret social interactions in both very similarly (while they continue to learn the distinction between the two).

Although Troy jokingly told us that parents need a guide to stalking their kids online, he spent a good bit of our time together describing how great of a job his wife has done simply by acting on her intuition. "She really trusts her gut instinct with the boys, and I've been super impressed. She's right *at least* nine times out of ten."

4. *USE A CONTENT BLOCKER … ONLY AS A BACKUP.* Various filters, blockers, and monitoring options can be helpful as a first strategy, but should never be our main strategy. Based on our discussions with parents, we have intentionally chosen not to recommend specific filters, blockers, or apps because this is a new and emerging market. For every new app teens start using, developers release new products and improve older platforms, and teenagers (and adults) start generating workarounds.

Janie gave an example of this: "The kids' school issued all the ninth graders laptops to use for the year. Allegedly they had a really good content filter on them. But within probably a week or two some kid in their class figured out how to disable it and told everybody else how to do it. So for basically that entire year, they all had these computers with no filters."

Our best advice is to **talk to parents you trust who have slightly older kids than yours** (and keep in mind that media use can vary between genders, so if you have boys, talk to a parent of other boys), as well as the parents of your kids' friends. You'll probably narrow your search to two or three options that you can then do a little more research about before choosing one.[15]

If you're in close relationship with a handful of families, it may also be helpful to ask all those families to agree on using a few of the same blockers or filters. These tools inevitably have weaknesses and drawbacks that both parents and kids discover as they use them. By agreeing to use the same software as your kids' friends, you can both alert and be alerted by other parents about any issues that might arise.

"We all want to think, 'Not my kid,' but once the hiding starts, it's easier to hide bigger things. Our kids know we can pick up their phones at any time, and they are fine with that. And if we find anything questionable, it doesn't have to be adversarial, it just means a discussion. There may be consequences if there is something that requires consequences, but it doesn't have to be a battle. My older son at one point told every one of his friends, 'My mom will pick up my phone or look at my messages at any time, so be careful what you send.'"

—DAWN, MOM OF THREE

5.  CREATE A PARENT RITUAL FOR CHECKING TEXTS AND SOCIAL SHARES. Among the parents we spoke with, virtually all of them talked about frequently looking through their kids' texts, chats, and profiles up to a certain age (which varied depending on each kid) to see what kinds of things they might find. One mom made a helpful observation about this type of monitoring: "The longer you wait in between checking, the more you have to dig through." As she started to appreciate this herself, she decided to make it a weekly ritual. "We sit down very comfortably, in a non-adversarial kind of way, and she just shows me what's going on in her life and what she's up to."

Alongside this, another helpful tip is to keep an eye on the types of advertising that come up while you're online on computers or logins you share. Many times kids will delete their browsing history, hoping to erase any record of where they've been. Companies that sell advertising online do so based on the sites that have been visited, whether or not the user deletes that history. Several parents told us that they found out something was up thanks to particular ads that caught their attention.

- - - - - - - - - - - - - - - - - - - - - - - - - - - - - - - - - - - - - - - - - - - - - - - - -

"Checking in on our daughter's phone was part of our agreement from the start. We said, 'This phone is our phone. There are times when I may need to use your phone or will check it. I want you to know that this is part of our agreement up front, so that you're not offended when I do it. If you lock your phone, that's good, but I need to know the password.'"

—KURT, DAD OF ONE

- - - - - - - - - - - - - - - - - - - - - - - - - - - - - - - - - - - - - - - - - - - - - - - - -

6. *BE THOUGHTFUL ABOUT ACCOUNT NAMES.*
Another strategy is to have kids use a pseudonym that is just a slight step away from their real name when they first begin using social media. One dad helped his son, who normally goes by J.T. Smith, set up a profile as John Thomas. This allowed the son to safely connect with friends and family, and possibly make some adolescent mistakes along the way, without harming J.T. Smith's reputation years down the road.

Similarly, parents might consider including the word "family" when they set up email accounts for their kids (e.g., art.bamford.family@website.com). The word "family" deters some solicitations and spam because it usually means that an entire family has access to an account rather than an individual.

Note that older teens may create accounts that use pseudonyms as a way to hide interactions with friends, or particular types of sharing, from their parents and other adults in their "public" network. It's important to talk with your kids about this and some of the negative impact of this kind of behavior, which we'll talk about more in chapter 5.

# DISCUSSION QUESTIONS

1 If you had to summarize your approach to the dangers of digital media mentioned in this chapter, would you say you typically use surveillance, supervision, something in between, or more of a hands-off approach?

2 What has worked well in your family so far when it comes to addressing online dangers and social media behavior? What hasn't been so successful?

3   After exploring the suggestions in the prior section, what one or two ideas would you like to talk with your kids about and experiment with together?

4   Based on what you've read, is there anything you want to add to your family covenant about how your family will both prevent and respond to some of these darker sides of digital media?

# 05

## HOW CAN I HELP MY KIDS BECOME GOOD DIGITAL CITIZENS

# I GUESS ANONYMITY MAKES PEOPLE MONSTERS[1]

## —ANONYMOUS TEENAGER

I came across this comment one day while researching a popular new app that "acts like a local bulletin board for your area" and lets users post anonymously.[2] Several schools in our community had recently banned this particular app, which I described to one parent as the "bathroom stall graffiti" of social media: Most of what I saw was goofing around, gossip, dirty jokes, and bragging about various illicit exploits.

But apparently it wasn't always that way. This comment was posted as part of a larger discussion lamenting how the well-intentioned app had started out as a therapeutic space where kids could be honest and vulnerable with one another and discuss their feelings in meaningful ways. But the freedom to share experiences and struggles had devolved into a free space to critique and slam others.

# IDENTIFY THE ISSUE

## HOW CAN I RAISE KIDS WHO WILL PARTICIPATE IN SOCIAL MEDIA THOUGHTFULLY AND RESPECTFULLY?

*Everything is amazing right now and nobody is happy.*
—Louis C.K.[3]

We have all come across adults who seem to vent their anger and frustrations from real life by sharing and posting online in ways that are obnoxious or even offensive to the rest of us. The most hate-filled of these folks are appropriately referred to as "Internet Trolls"—anonymous users who post nasty, mean comments in forums and user comment sections for their own amusement. The nickname fits because they can make the Internet an ugly, unhappy place for the rest of us.

There are even more "typical" Internet users who seem to indulge themselves by behaving in less offensive or obnoxious, but equally self-absorbed, ways. Carrie, a mom of three, pretty aptly described Facebook to us as a "Brag Book" and explained, "We adults use social media to tell the whole world that our families are successful. We use it to brag and show off, and I think the kids imitate that in their own ways."

She makes a great point here. Remember our discussion about uses and gratifications in chapter 2? **When kids see adults using media to feel better about themselves, they're likely to follow that example.** They may use different sites and apps to do so, but often they are satisfying the same underlying needs and desires.

Sadly, adults have set a pretty lousy example for kids when it comes to online etiquette. We've created an "anything goes" atmosphere that often feels like a race to the bottom.

Researchers have called this free-for-all the *online disinhibition effect*.[4] Adults use digital media to behave and interact in all sorts of ways that they never would in real life. And for some reason our society seems to have reached a consensus that this is okay (and dissenters feel rather powerless to do anything about it).

As Christian parents, this is one area where we need to be clear with our kids—and live by example. No, it is not okay to be haughty, rude, hateful, combative, perverted, or obscene just because we're online.

The reality with digital natives is that they start out behaving *very* consistently between their on and offline lives. Then they use digital spaces to play with their identities as they work out the important question, "Who am I?" But at some point as young people settle into their own unique identities, they begin to recognize that online disinhibition is the status quo.[5] Teens begin to see online environments as places for cathartic bad behavior, where anonymity can make us monsters.

In wrestling with this question about digital citizenship, we're hoping to pin down answers that help us both as digital citizens in a global community *and* as people who belong, first and foremost, to God's kingdom.

We want our kids to learn how to love their neighbors and live out their faith online as well as off. But what does that even look like? How can we help our kids to get into the habit of being salt and light, and ambassadors for God's kingdom in the digital world?

# REFRAME OUR VIEW

## *AUTOPSY OF AN ONLINE TROLL*

"My son Peter got in the car one day, handed me his phone, and said 'I don't want it.' I couldn't believe it. There was so much drama and people being mean to each other that he was just sick of it. I was pretty surprised."

This was an encouraging moment for Peter's mom, Sydney. Although her son was frustrated, she couldn't help but be proud of him for being disgusted and walking away rather than joining the fray with his peers.

In order for us to begin dismantling the myth that "anything goes" online, we need to understand how that myth came into existence. So far we have described a host of ways that digital media has become a new expression of activities that young people have always done on playgrounds or in cafeterias. Yet digital media is also unique from "real" life in certain ways that make it tempting to behave differently.

Researchers have identified four interconnected attributes of digital media spaces that foster the kind of aggressive, troll-like behavior that drove Peter away from wanting to participate. As parents, we need to be aware of these key characteristics and discuss them with our kids.

# 1. DIGITAL CONTENT FEELS NON-PERMANENT

"I HATE YOU!"

I'm not proud to admit that I once said this to my dad, but I'll confess that in a moment of teen-brain emotional overload, I did. (Sorry, Dad! Love you!) But while I may have blurted this out during a heated moment, I never would have written it, recorded it, or shared it publicly. It was impulsive, and it felt wrong the moment it left my mouth.

We very instinctively perceive *speaking* differently from what we choose to capture using media. We learn to assume that expressions through writing, photos, and video are more permanent and potentially public, so we're typically more thoughtful about choosing what we share, and how, than when we talk.[6]

As digital immigrants, adults tend to skew more toward this type of mindfulness when we use digital media, too. **But just like our kids learn to speak before they write, digital natives initially approach online interaction much more like speech**. They only learn over time—through experience—what it means for something to be permanent or have consequences that go beyond what they expected.

Telling kids that someone will someday look back through everything they've ever done online is a bit like telling them their metabolism is going to slow down. We know for certain it's true, but for teenagers it's like, "Um, okay. Whatever." We can warn kids, but it is a lesson that typically demands some experience to be understood. As a result, trotting out this particular motif in one of our "lectures" on social media can cue kids to tune out altogether.[7]

It would be nice if we could protect young people from having to learn the hard way about digital content being permanent simply by warning them. The reality we heard from a lot of parents was that their kids needed to experience this somehow, first or secondhand, before the lesson really stuck. Sydney told us, "There was an incident at their school where a girl shared a video of herself engaged in some sexual acts. The video itself was shared around school pretty quickly, and our kids witnessed the fallout from that and learned from it. It's too bad that's what it takes a lot of times for kids to learn—one of them has to go through something like that."

Because of the type of relationship Sydney had built with her kids, they shared what had happened with Sydney, giving her a springboard to talk about how what we post can become permanent. Their classmate's struggle finally drove home a point about digital content that Sydney had been trying to teach them for months.

# 2. DIGITAL USERS CAN APPEAR ANONYMOUS

One of the trickiest aspects of navigating digital media for both kids and adults is the issue of anonymity. On the one hand, it can be fun to put on a costume and play with a new identity. But at a certain point, we need to mature past wanting to play dress-up.

Adults are often emboldened by anonymity, and usually not in a good way. Masks become something we knowingly hide behind to conceal who we really are. When thinking with your kids about identity, it may be helpful to use the categories of *avatars*, *costumes*, and our *authentic selves*.

**AVATARS** —Used to play games, avatars represent us in fictional worlds.

**COSTUMES** —Used by kids to play, we put costumes on in the real world to alter or conceal our identity.

**AUTHENTIC SELVES** —Expressed in our everyday lives, our "real" self is a continually evolving interaction between how we perceive ourselves and how we imagine others perceive us.

It can be difficult for teenagers and young adults, still in the process of forming their identities, to switch between these modes as easily as adults do. The way they interface with digital media makes it hard to distinguish when they're playing as an avatar, participating in a costume, or just showing up as themselves.

# 3. DIGITAL INTERACTIONS SEEM TO LACK CONSEQUENCES

The third of these troll-like characteristics is pretty obvious. Regardless of whether something will be permanent or perhaps anonymous, we pause to weigh any negative outcomes we may experience later against the more immediate positives. Digital media easily deceives us into thinking that there will be no tangible, substantial consequences from our posts.

This is why it is good to engage as much as possible with kids about what they're doing online. It helps them develop an internal sense that others are paying attention, not just when they happen to make a mistake or get caught.

With digital media we must be clear that we are concerned with how our kids interact with others, which has real consequences. Unlike analog media, this is not just a matter of what they are doing "under our roof" according to our rules and expectations. When kids act out online, the consequences extend beyond their family and home.

# 4. BAD BEHAVIOR IS THE STATUS QUO

This last characteristic of trolling is where our kids deserve an apology from adults.

**Researchers have found that increasingly as teens get older, they begin to recognize the "anything goes" ethos that adults have established online and start acting accordingly.** They assume, following the example adults have set, that it is "normal" to check their ethics and morals at the door when entering digital spaces.[8]

If you're like us, you hope your kids will be different as followers of Jesus. This means we have to move beyond the question about what *not* to do online as Christians and instead ask: How do we *want* to behave and interact?

- - - - - - - - - - - - - - - - - - - - - - - - - - - - - - - - - - - - - - -

"Context seems to go out the window with digital media. People post, say, comment on, friend, and engage in ways that would be considered appalling in real life interaction. It's a real challenge."

*—ALEX, DAD OF THREE*

- - - - - - - - - - - - - - - - - - - - - - - - - - - - - - - - - - - - - - -

# NAME THE GOAL

## *AUTHENTICITY AND EMPATHY*

*No one gossips about other people's secret virtues.*
—Bertrand Russell[9]

When it comes to our kids' engagement as digital citizens, we are wise to focus on two key traits: authenticity and empathy. These virtues are the hinges on which questions of "Can I?" become "I can, but do I *want* to?"

# AUTHENTICITY

Our biblical commandment against lying does not say, "Thou shalt not lie," even though that's how we're prone to remember it. Exodus 20:16 actually warns: "You shall not give false testimony against your neighbor." This image of a person testifying to their side of a story before a jury of peers alerts us to how truth-telling isn't just "saying the right words." It is an embodied practice that happens in relationships, embedded within social networks. It has consequences not only for us, but also for our neighbors, friends, and even strangers with whom we cross paths.

Sydney, the mom we mentioned earlier, gave a great definition of authenticity as she described their family: **"We're the kind of people who don't really have a home personality and then a public persona**, which has always been clear to our kids. They just know who we are."

Thanks to digital media, we now "exist" as public citizens much more three-dimensionally in front of a vastly greater number of people. Our identities and reputations are an aggregate of text, photos, videos, and carefully cultivated network profiles. We have tons of options and a lot more control when it comes to managing our presence online, but that shouldn't be taken as an opportunity to manufacture a virtual reality that is something foreign to who we really are.

Authenticity means being able to share and participate without caring too much about what others think. This shouldn't be done in a flippant, disrespectful way, but **with a sense of confidence that our identities are rooted in and find their meaning in Christ.**

Being authentic also means we don't fall into the common trap of overinflating how much "fun" our family is having, or what "great" experiences we are sharing with our kids. As one grandmother observed to us, "I spend a lot of time with my daughters-in-law and my grandchildren. I love them all dearly, but after I spend a day with them, I check out what my daughters-in-law have posted on social media. What really happened is a far cry from the 'sweetness and light' that they project online."

One of the best strategies we heard from parents for teaching kids to participate more authentically was to have them connect first with Christian adults and friends when they initially began using social media. Some of these parents kept kids limited to these types of friends for a while; others used them simply to seed the ground.

Helping kids connect with folks who seem to share and participate authentically, like Carrie and her kids, models healthy engagement and makes negative behaviors seem like exceptions rather than the rule. Even if some of the Christian adults your kids connect with *don't* model authenticity that well, this strategy will raise their level of self-awareness about what they're sharing, which can be helpful while they are younger (though be aware that for older kids this might feel like surveillance).

Another parent told us that he and his wife made a point of having an ongoing dialogue with their kids about how they were presenting themselves online, and whether or not that lined up with who they were offline. By doing this, they were able to join their kids in using social media as a tool in the identity formation process.

# EMPATHY

*The best guiding principle is to always cherish individuals first.*
—Jaron Lanier[10]

One of the most difficult things to teach kids, and remember ourselves, is that there are real people with emotions, needs, desires, and disappointments beneath our screens and behind the networks in which we participate. Our actions in digital spaces may not seem permanent or have consequences from our point of view, but that doesn't mean they won't impact others in significant, lasting ways offline.

Sydney told us that she made a habit of commenting out loud on what she saw people sharing while her kids were within ear shot. "I'll read or describe what one of my friends has posted, when they're totally oversharing, and say, 'Why is she sharing this? Who cares?' I hope that my daughter hears that and realizes that people are reacting to what she posts too."

Carrie sent a screenshot of her son's social media post to him with the question, "Really?" when he was being disingenuous about something. This allowed her to comment on what Rob shared without committing the *ultimate* no-no: actually posting publicly on her teen son's profile.

By the time he was a senior, Rob gave his mom a taste of her own medicine: "I posted a photo of our daughter on a mission trip because I thought she looked really cute playing with these adorable little kids. Rob came in and saw it, and pointed at it and said, 'Mom, we're not going to be the kind of family that uses this for bragging now, right? That's not who we are.' And I said, 'No, you're right.' Frankly I was irked because I really did like the photo, but he busted me for using it as a place to brag. I was proud of him for catching that."

———————————————————————————————————————— [○]

Don't force or obligate kids to participate with you and other family members publicly on social media. The goal is for them to share authentically and interact with empathy for others. In fact, it's a good idea to regularly check in with your kids face to face by asking, "How do you feel about how much I'm interacting with you on social media? Do you wish it was less or more?" Be ready for the honest answer! Parents commenting directly—positively or negatively—on social media is often seen as intrusive to teenagers.

# RIGHT CLICK

## [DIGITAL] CHRISTIANS

A fantastic question for families to talk about is: "What does it mean to be a digital Christian?" Kids will likely tell you what you want to hear at first: Don't use bad words or go to inappropriate websites. But push the question past what we *don't* do:

- How can we be peacemakers or peacekeepers on social media?

- How can we use our online anonymity to be a blessing to strangers, like a superhero in disguise rather than a troll? Encourage your kids to make an anonymous gift online or post an affirming comment on something, and talk to them about how it makes them feel and how they imagine someone on the receiving end will feel.

- Explain the parallels between our offline ethics and online practices. Why do we feel it is important to purchase and download music when we could have it for free instead?

- How can we affirm and build up friends and peers publicly on social media or privately through a text or chat? Simple acts of kindness are often just as appreciated online as in person.

◎ What does it look like to share and celebrate good news with friends rather than bragging or showing off? Talk with your kids about when it is okay to share something that might feel like bragging.

◎ How do you weigh in on issues of social justice, using social media to engage issues important to you? What does it look like to reflect your faith in the ways you respond or call others to action?

◎ After church services, ask kids how they could share their takeaways on social media using images rather than words (which sounds like a challenge to us, but probably won't be for them).

◎ Share and discuss any Christian apps you use. Almost all of the parents in one of our focus groups said they regularly used some Bible study apps, but *none* had recommended or installed any of these tools onto their kids' phones! One dad looked away from our table with a stricken expression and quietly said to himself, "I *can't believe* I didn't download the Bible on their phones." Just seeing an app icon with a cross or Bible on it can be a helpful, frequent reminder regardless of whether or not kids use it. For younger teens, arrange the icons on your kids' home screens so that these apps are near the ones they use most often!

# SHOULD I FRIEND/FOLLOW MY KIDS' FRIENDS?

We discovered that most parents are trying to figure this one out in real-time with their kids. One of the more helpful standards we heard was from a couple who shared, "We do not friend, but we will accept friend requests. That way our kids' friends are initiating rather than us. We've even asked our kids if accepting certain friend requests is okay with them." These same parents discovered that photography was one role the teenagers in their life wanted the parents to play. The mom routinely takes pictures before events like school dances. "After every dance, she posts a whole album of pictures from the pre-dance photo shoot (usually with our girls' permission). The girls, and their friends, love them and appreciate the care she took to capture the moment." But even this role is part of an ongoing dialogue in their family about what kind of interaction feels right, and in what social media spaces.

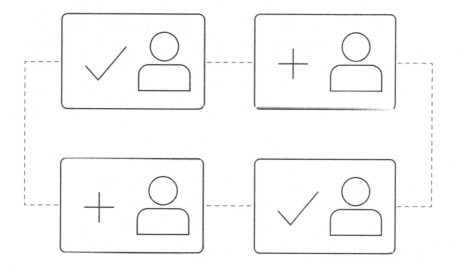

# DISCUSSION QUESTIONS

1    When you think about authenticity and empathy expressed online, what does that look like? Do any people come to mind who strike you as being able to convey these traits (or not) through how they interact through digital media?

2    What are some of the most positive, affirming experiences you've had involving media, such as someone sending you an encouraging note? Write down several people who you might similarly encourage using digital media in the next few weeks, and talk with your kids about how best to do so.

3   If your teens use social media, look through some of their posts and identify the ones you see as being the most authentic representations of who they are, or who they were during an earlier phase of their development. Talk with them about why you like certain things they have shared as expressions of their identity. Ask them to do the same with what you have shared.

4   Given your family dreams about being good digital citizens, what would you like to add to your family covenant?

# 06

## HOW (AND WHEN) CAN I GRACEFULLY TAKE OFF THE MEDIA TRAINING WHEELS?

# "OUR SON MADE A TOTALLY ASININE DECISION ..."

Lauren began telling us about a prank her fifteen-year-old son pulled on a female friend.

"He saw this idea on a website somewhere. He posed online as this girl and posted her contact info on a video chatting app with a comment that said, 'Hey guys, send me a picture of your you-know-what at this account and I'll tell you if I like it or not.' He thought she would get a few responses and think, 'Oh this is gross,' or whatever. But she got, like, *hundreds* of them in about ten minutes."

Whether you're Lauren in this scenario or you're the parents of the girl on the receiving end of the prank, this story probably confirms many of your parental fears. We worry about the immediate consequences of a stunt like this for sure. We wonder what longer-term consequences might trail either of these kids into the future.

We're also anxious about what kind of trouble our kids might get into once they leave home. How can we be sure they won't completely blow it with social media interactions as young adults?

# IDENTIFY THE ISSUE

## WE WANT TO GUIDE OUR TEENAGERS TOWARD DIGITAL MATURITY, BUT WE AREN'T SURE HOW

Like us, you may be wondering: **How can I help my teenagers navigate digital media responsibly now, so that when the training wheels come off, they're ready?** After all, we parents are not always going to be around to peek at their texts every day or collect their devices every night.

The ultimate goals of healthy boundaries, stronger relationships, and authenticity can play out differently with each of our children. Maybe your youngest son will struggle with boundaries at fourteen, whereas your eldest daughter will grapple with authenticity at eighteen. Both our kids and digital technology continue to grow and change each day. This is yet another reason why digital media has been such a challenge for us as parents.

**We want to have fair, consistent rules for each of our kids. But they don't use the same media or use it the same ways.** Like one dad told us, "We didn't let our older son use Facebook until he was probably sixteen or seventeen, but with our younger daughter it was the primary mode of communication from the directors at her theatre group. We felt like we had no choice but to let her join at thirteen. Now she's sixteen and doesn't even use Facebook anymore."

So to restate our question for this chapter more precisely: As *each one of our kids* gets older and more mature, how can we slowly allow more freedom and responsibility *according to his or her own unique needs and interests?* This requires also asking: *How should we respond when our kids make bad decisions with digital media?*

## DISASTER PREPAREDNESS: *HOW TO RESPOND WHEN SOMETHING REALLY BAD HAPPENS*

When I first moved from the Midwest to California, I was given instructions on what to do, and a list of supplies to keep around, in case there was ever a severe earthquake. Of course the hope is that I'll never *need* to use any of it, but knowing good safety protocols can be as helpful for adults in intense moments as they are for kids. They also provide some peace of mind.

There are a variety of ways young people might screw up in seriously bad ways using social media that similarly could shake your family's world. Throughout this book, we have included examples from a few real scenarios that parents graciously shared with us, but we also wanted to specifically answer this question: **If it happens to your family, what can you do?**

Here are six basic steps you might take in the immediate fallout from a digital disaster, distilled from our conversations with parents who have been there. Ideally you'll never need this list, but it is good to have it filed away, just in case.

1. **Take a deep breath and count to ten**—Seriously. When teens make bad decisions using digital media, it often has more to do with lack of impulse control than lack of character. If they had stopped to think before sharing, they wouldn't have shared. The problem is they don't often stop to think. This is actually developmentally appropriate for an adolescent, not a deep flaw of your particular child. As tough as this may be, it is important that parents try to model a bit of restraint by reclaiming our cool before we react.

**2. Assess the content situation**—A lot of social media mistakes we heard about involved sharing inappropriate content. In some cases it was between two teens, and in other cases it spread to the whole school (and beyond). **Because digital content can be shared so quickly, it is not enough to have your son or daughter delete something from a personal device.** Figure out how far the content in question may have spread. For example, if your daughter sent something inappropriate to her boyfriend, you'll want to speak with the boyfriend's parents and figure out if he shared what she sent with any friends. Don't assume that all digital content goes from zero to viral instantaneously. It is possible that just one, five, or ten other kids have a copy of something. But the sooner you begin to contain the flow, the better.

**3. Contact other parents**—While you're trying to assess the situation, and as you're trying to stop content from spreading any further online, don't hesitate to contact the other parents involved. Be honest and let them know you are trying to handle the situation, and talk through what seems appropriate for all parties. Try to do this as congenially as possible, and don't let your embarrassment stall you. These conversations must happen now. Welcome to parenting teenagers in a digital world. **You're better off making calls ASAP than waiting to receive them.**

**4. Reach out to school, church, and (if necessary) police**—All of us are in the midst of new kinds of problems that arise from digital media use. Several parents we spoke with told us that they reached out to their kids' school for support, called their youth pastor, or even drove to the local police department to figure out what they should do (especially

### DISASTER PREPAREDNESS: *HOW TO RESPOND WHEN SOMETHING REALLY BAD HAPPENS*

when the situation involved sharing nude images). **Many of these folks understand where you're coming from, deal with similar questions often, and will be as supportive as possible.** Unfortunately, a lot of educators, pastors, and friends in law enforcement we asked about this said they felt underutilized by parents from their church and in their community.

5. **Make sure the punishment fits the crime**—Gossip at schools has shifted from "Did you hear?" to "Have you seen?" You may very well catch your son or daughter with something very scandalous or explicit on their device. Before you freak out, figure out why it's there. Some kids may receive the latest gossip image and keep it simply for the sake of feeling included. That doesn't make it okay, but it is quite different from being the one who took the photo, shot the video, or appeared in a photo or video. Let your kids know that you "get" this and want to be reasonable, while also upholding your family's standards for what is appropriate. The conversation you need to have might be about which friends they're connected with, and how they feel about what's being shared between friends, in addition to their own behavior.

When your son or daughter is the instigator of the content, talk with them about what they think reasonable discipline might look like. Taking away devices or online privileges for a season is often the most appropriate response. Making private or public apologies might also be important, especially if something was shared that caused real or potential damage to another student or a group of peers. Commit to stand with your child as they make these apologies, and keep reminding them (and yourself!) that this mistake is not the end of the world. Center these conversations in your love and support, and in God's relentless grace. *Jesus is bigger than any mistake!* He can handle digital media failure.

6. **Get behind the behavior to the real issues**—Sometimes this type of behavior can be sheer adolescent development in action, complete with a lack of future thinking or regard for consequences. But inappropriate or destructive behavior can also be a way of getting grown-ups to pay attention. It is easy to think that once the situation has been handled and some type of punishment has been put in place, our parenting job is done. In reality, it may only be the Band-Aid on the wound.

   If you take away your son or daughter's digital media privileges, take the opportunity to reconnect with them and figure out how they're actually doing. One dad told us he was shocked to discover that his daughter was suffering from depression. She had shared inappropriate texts, and he had taken her phone away for a while. He realized, "Media actually hid her depression from us. We drew too much from it and inferred things from what she posted." They missed the warning signs that emerged once her social media self stepped offstage.

# REFRAME OUR VIEW

## ARCHITECT, MENTOR, AND COMPANION

There are three modes we should shift between when it comes to teaching our kids about media: *architect, mentor,* and *companion.*

## 1. ARCHITECT.

This mode is best when our instincts tell us that the precious kids with whom we have been entrusted need our protection. We're the adults; they're the children. So we create and uphold a scaffolding of rules, rituals, and boundaries designed to protect them and help them learn how to build their own lives someday. These often become like a set of blueprints. But like John Lennon once sang, "Life is what happens to you while you're busy making other plans."[1] So we try our best to stick to these structures while continuing to adapt and amend them as our kids grow up.

In Lauren's case, she and her husband took away their son's Internet access for several weeks as punishment for his prank—including his use for school, which surprised us. Lauren responded, "Oh yeah, we called the school and said, 'Look, we need to keep him offline a while. He totally screwed up, and this is how we need to correct him.' They were supportive of the decision, and they sent us the homework or printed it for him. The school loved it."

**As architects, we reserve the right to take devices away and turn them off, as needed, until our kids are eighteen. Don't forget that.** We also reserve the right to stop paying their technology-related bills at any point (before or after age eighteen). While some fifteen-year-olds are earning their own money to pay for a phone, an awful lot of late twenty-somethings remain on their parents' phone plan, which should raise some important questions for us as a culture. Sometimes the simple act of paying their own bills helps young people wise up about tech usage.

## 2. MENTOR.

We become mentors when we thoughtfully engage with kids about how they use media in order to teach them lessons and skills that will serve them later in life. As caring adults, we try to share some of the wisdom we have accumulated over the years through experience. Much of what we have encouraged in this book is simply more mentor-mode engagement with digital media— parents and kids thinking together about the role these new tools play in our lives.

In addition to taking away his Internet, Lauren and her husband talked *a lot* with their son about what he did and why. "He ended up confessing a ton of other stuff and said, 'I've been hiding who I am from you guys.' He also said, 'I don't agree with a lot of your rules, and I know you don't approve of a lot of what I've been doing, but I'll try to be more respectful.' We actually had him start counselling as a result, which has helped all of us."

As Lauren described the fallout from this incident, she got a bit choked up. "I actually called the mom [of the girl who was pranked] back a few weeks later to thank her. I said 'thank you' because *I got my kid back*. We believe in a God who is redemptive and works through our mistakes, and he sure did with this one. God makes beautiful things happen through all the crap sometimes. My kids are the oldest in our group of friends, and when the other parents ask me I always tell them, 'You're going to make mistakes; your kids will *definitely* make a ton of mistakes. So you either believe in a God who is redemptive or not.'" Mentors always look for the hopeful angle.

### 3. COMPANION.

Lauren's faithful perseverance throughout her son's struggles is a helpful lead-in to our third mode: *companion*. Sometimes we hang out with our kids and use media *with* them for fun, to relax, and increasingly to communicate and keep in touch. **As our kids get older and mature into young adults, our relationship shifts; this mode begins to eclipse the other two and moves to the forefront of how we interact.**

Of course this is not to say we *ever* stop occasionally flipping back into architect mode to help our grown-up kids collaboratively problem-solve, or mentor mode to offer some advice, but as our kids age, our bond with them eventually centers around the relationship we share rather than obligation or responsibility.

For Lauren's family, media had become like a wedge driving their son farther and farther away. His colossal screwup helped open their eyes to some bigger issues, and his consequences (several weeks without digital media) allowed them to make big strides back toward common ground.

# YOU'VE GOT A FRIEND IN MEDIA

Shifting into this adult companionship phase is a bit like a dance when our kids are teenagers. We guide them one step forward toward freedom, then one step back toward responsibility. It's one step forward with a trial, another step back to work through errors.

**What makes this dance so tricky for parents is that, at some point, the song changes.** Rules and restrictions can have a lot of benefits for children up to a certain stage in their development, but as they move into late adolescence, restrictions begin to feel more and more like we're stepping on their toes. Media scholar Lynn Schofield Clark explains that our restrictions can "seem to encourage teens to engage in more secretive behavior, making [them] more likely to engage in forbidden actions ... when they are out of their parents' purview."[2]

As our kids get older and we begin to think about their transition out of the home, it is important to think about how we juggle these three parental modes. For example, we can begin to mutually address more minor issues, like looking at a text in the middle of a face-to-face conversation, *with* our kids as companions. And in a reciprocal way, we listen when they point out some of these behaviors to us without jumping into a defensive "I'm the parent" mode.

We might also begin to better recognize and accept how media will be a part of their future vocations. As adults, our media use varies quite a bit depending on our profession, relationships, and interests outside of work. If your seventeen-year-old seems to use digital media more than her peers, but does so in a non-secretive way that feels okay to you, it might just be her first steps on the path toward a career or hobby. A member of my church's youth group used to constantly create and share goofy videos online. He's starting college next fall with a scholarship in media and journalism thanks to all those quirky clips (which apparently got more views and likes than we realized).

# WIRELESS PARENTING ⊣ ///// ⊢

The adolescent phase of development seems to have extended in recent years, which some scholars have, in part, attributed to what they describe as the "digital tether."[3] **When Mom and Dad are always just a text message away and continue to monitor their kids' social media, many young people struggle to gain a feeling of independence as emerging adults.** Today's parents know way more about what kids are doing, not only while they're growing up but also after they have left home. This can lead to a lot of anxiety that previous generations of parents never had ... and with what benefit? Clark has argued that this sort of "intrusiveness can backfire and can contribute to raising overly dependent and self-focused young people."[4]

**When it comes to raising kids who will become healthy adults, we must allow enough freedom so that our kids can learn resilience, self-regulation, and responsibility for themselves.**

As teens get older, we model what it looks like for digital media to be part of adult friendships and careers. Our kids might make bad decisions, but our response mode changes. Rather than defaulting to "you just lost phone privileges for two days" kinds of rule enforcement that might have worked with thirteen-year-olds, it is crucial to develop with later adolescents what one mom described as "an open, ongoing conversation about *their* decisions." Young people need to learn, sometimes through mistakes, that what they choose to do with digital media has consequences.

One dad told us that he actually appreciated digital media for this reason. "When our daughter's classmates act out, a lot of that is shared publicly now, and she sees it. I remember going to a party when I was younger and everybody was smoking and drinking and it was like, 'Whoa, what do I do now?' I can't imagine our daughter being ambushed like that, because she knows who those kids are and what's going on from social media. She's actually brought concerns about that stuff to us before rather than after situations happen. That, to me, is great. **I would much rather have those conversations** *before* **she encounters something in real life because she has seen it online."**

## NAME THE GOAL

### *ACCOUNTABILITY*

If we're being totally honest, one of our biggest worries as parents is that our kids will end up using digital media a lot like we do, in some of the ways that bother us. They'll feel perpetually interrupted, struggle to be present and attentive, wish they made more time to enjoy things like a good book or coffee with a friend without constantly checking their phone, or feel unsatisfied with their life compared to what they see in their social media feeds.

**So the real question is: How well are we using** *our own* **freedom and responsibility with digital media?** How can we help our kids and help ourselves at the same time? Parents often use the language of *addiction* to discuss how young people use digital media, but rarely do we use the language of *recovery*. While addiction language is probably too strong to describe how most of us use technology, nevertheless the first step toward changing any behavior is admitting that we have a problem.[5]

**APP CHAT** -----------------------------------------

Many parents we interviewed were challenged by the rate at which their kids were downloading and trying out new apps. **How can we quickly evaluate and make decisions about apps on the fly while also equipping our kids to learn to think about and navigate new apps themselves?**

First, you want to try to quickly nail down a few key issues: privacy, anonymity, and appropriate sharing/behavior. App descriptions give you some of this information, but you want to read it for yourself after you've discovered what your son or daughter already knows (or thinks they know).

Here are five questions to discuss with kids when they ask about a new app:

1. Why do you want it? (What does it do? Which of your friends are using it?)

2. What kind of privacy will you have? How much personal information will you be sharing with others and with the app?

3. Will you be using this app as yourself, as an avatar, or as an anonymous user, and why?

4. What kind of interaction or sharing are you hoping to do?

5. What do you think would be considered appropriate or inappropriate use of this app?

Ask your kids to walk you through all of this while you're looking at the description page in the app store. Check for the developer's recommended user age, read a few customer reviews, and see what kind of personal information users are required to provide. Watch for the phrase "in-app purchases" as well—this means users can pay for upgrades after the app has been downloaded. You may also want to do a quick search on a site like commonsensemedia.org where other parents are rating and reviewing apps and games.

And remember: You're the parent. It's totally appropriate to say, "Give me twenty-four hours to think about this," or "I need to find out a little bit more about this one," or simply, "Nope. Not that app."

It can also be worthwhile to download and try an app yourself. Recently a friend at church asked me about a new one his kids wanted to use. I downloaded it, used it for a while, and was able to tell him what I saw as pros and cons. Of course, the moment his kids learned that I used the app incognito, they lost all interest in joining. Dad was pleased!

"Texting and driving, or even just phone usage while driving with my kids, is a daily question for me. I try to say things like, 'I need to use navigation right now,' but realize that I absolutely wouldn't want them to do what I do when they start to drive—yikes!"

—AI, MOM OF TWO

# PARTNER WITH YOUR KIDS IN YOUR OWN GOALS

Perhaps the best thing we can do with teens is partner *with* them, working collaboratively to address habits or behaviors that we struggle with ourselves. As our kids get older, they need to move from having rules and limits imposed on them to learning how to make and keep standards as adults. They need to be included in conversations about how to set boundaries and accountability structures together in relationships and as a family.

This is especially true if we ourselves struggle with boundaries.

**There is no shame in admitting that we aren't happy with some of the ways we use digital media or the role it has come to play in our lives.** We might wish we took more breaks from social media or that we felt like we could turn off our phones overnight.

But as we try to rein in our own behaviors, we often fail to appreciate that our kids can be our biggest allies! Think about it:

- Young people are in a much more flexible and adaptable stage of life than ours.

- Today's young people value authenticity as much as ever.[6]

- Teens treasure moments when they feel respected as a young man or woman rather than protected as a child, shuffled away to the kids' table.

- Our kids are often our biggest fans! It helps to have someone you love rooting for you as you seek to change.

Invite kids to hold you accountable for limits you set for yourself—they'll appreciate a chance to return the favor! I've told my kids that when they come into the room when I'm working from home, I want to shut my laptop and give them my full focus. I probably do that seventy-five percent of the time, and when I don't, my kids will sometimes say with a grin on their face, "Mom, you need to shut your laptop." They enjoy helping me with a goal I've told them about, and I'm grateful for the reminders that talking face-to-face with them is way more important than emptying my inbox. Not only that, but almost without exception, *they* are more important than whoever has emailed me.

"I have explained to my kids that I have separate emails for work and home, and my work email does not come to my phone. Once I am home, work can't invade unless I invite it in. I also check my personal email before they get up, while they are doing homework, and after they go to bed. They know I'm making a conscious effort to create these boundaries, so if at times I do have to respond to something work-related when I'm with them, it's the exception rather than the rule, and it's usually no big deal to them."

*—DALE, DAD OF TWO*

# EMPOWER YOUR TEENAGERS TO CREATE THEIR OWN BOUNDARIES

Once your teenagers seem to be settling into their own rhythms and routines with digital media, give them opportunities to establish their own boundaries. Then evaluate those boundaries together.

One mom described this in terms of being like "the bumper rails at the bowling alley." For example, let's say you have a rule that your kids may not add any friends to a social media network that they have not first met face-to-face. Here's how a couple who had that rule described what happened as their kids got older: "We phased it out by about sophomore year; they connected with some friends of friends at other schools. We could still trace all their connections back to one of those people they met face-to-face, and most of the strangers are geographically close by. It's like the degrees of separation thing, which seems pretty natural." Eventually the bumpers give way to the gutters, but by that point, young people are well aware of the potential dangers of slipping off track.

# KEEP TALKING TOGETHER

Include your kids in conversations about how they as individuals and the family as a whole are doing with digital media. These conversations are helpful before or during vacations, or to set common expectations for day-to-day media use. But the key element of these conversations is that you aren't simply dictating the rules; you're working together to listen to and appreciate each person's perspective before creating a shared understanding.

## RIGHT CLICK

*GROWING UP DIGITAL*

Near the end of our interview with Lauren, she offered the following reflection:

"I imagine if Jesus were alive today, he would have shared a parable that **faith is like parenting a fourteen-year-old. You hope everything is going to work out okay, but most of the time you're thinking, 'I'm not so sure about this.'**"

She's right. As we interviewed parents for this book, many were anxious about the challenges of raising good kids in today's rapidly changing world. But some of these parents, especially those whose kids are in their later teens, hold this anxiety in balance with another truth from Ecclesiastes 1:9– "There is nothing new under the sun." They now realize that many of their fears centering on digital media were just new manifestations of more basic parental concerns about the physical, emotional, and spiritual well-being of their kids.

We want to leave you with five big-picture takeaways as you migrate the contents of this book into your family's everyday life:

# 1. TALK ABOUT MEDIA—A LOT.

Digital media isn't going away. Rather than either keeping media use private or pretending like it's the enemy, make your home a place where families share, interact, and enjoy media together. There are certain things we typically only do at home, like sleeping, showering, and getting dressed. Teach kids that, while people use devices privately out in public, home is a place where loved ones talk safely and candidly about what we're doing and experiencing with digital media, as part of our real lives rather than a virtual "other" world.

Some families we interviewed were more or less strict than our own, and others were more pro- or anti-technology than we are. Regardless of the differences, we heard again and again that an ample amount of honest communication about digital media is hugely important. Start early and be intentional about keeping conversations going—especially as you begin gradually allowing more and more freedom for older teenagers. **Just as important as what you say is how often you talk with your kids about digital media.**

One parent shared, "We've tried to make technology part of normal conversation. My middle schooler recently told us about her friend who has two of every social media account—one that her parents monitor and one that they don't know about. My daughter inherently knew that sounded wrong, and she felt like it was safe to ask us about it."

## 2. INVEST TIME IN *YOUR* SOCIAL NETWORK.

Another common theme in our interviews was how valuable support networks are in helping parents engage the challenges they face with digital media.

You might have noticed in Lauren's story that she called the mother whose daughter had been pranked by her son. They were friends. The two families were able to adequately deal with that situation together without any major collateral damage (like a lawsuit, school suspension, or arrest) for either of their kids.

We heard a number of stories like Lauren's, several of which you've already seen as examples in earlier chapters, where kids totally blew it using digital media but parents were able to work together with other parents to resolve the situation. Kids can and will learn many of the valuable lessons they need to learn about privacy, anonymity, and appropriate sharing within a safe network of people you know and trust before stepping out and connecting with the bigger world out there. This can only happen as you invest in your support network.

"The biggest thing we've done," Cassandra, a mom from California, told us, "and I think the best investment, has been in the relationships we keep with other parents. This has gotten tougher as they get older, but I still try to connect as best I can with other parents."

## 3. DON'T LET COMPARISON STEAL YOUR JOY.

Working with a network of other parents doesn't mean every family has to use digital media in the same ways. As one mom told us, "We've been very willing to say, 'I don't care what anybody else thinks.'" It is tough not to fall into the comparison trap. We all wonder how we stack up against other families— perhaps you've wondered that even as you've read about families in this book. But digital media is simply not a level playing field. Gone are the days when limiting kids to X number of hours engaging with "age-appropriate content" made you a "good" parent. We're swimming in a muddy creek.

Honestly, that's good news. **Other parents can be resources and allies rather than points of comparison or competitors.** When it comes to digital media, no two families are going to do everything exactly alike, which makes comparison fairly futile.

## 4. DO NOT BE AFRAID.

Our fears and anxieties about digital media can confuse kids while they're younger and can become invitations to use media as a way of rebelling when they're teens. Being honest and humble enough to work with our kids when it comes to questions about digital media can go a long way.

Simply put, kids aren't stupid. At the beginning of this book, we explained how this is a transitional phase in which our culture is negotiating how to incorporate all sorts of new technology into our lives. Many young people get that and are thinking about it just like we are. They know where their expertise outstrips our own, and they recognize how technology gets in the way of meaningful relationships, even if they seem oblivious at times. It is crucial for parents to be willing to take a few steps out of *our* comfort zones in order to meet kids in the middle and work with them.

# 5. AT THE END OF THE DAY, LAUGH.

*Laughter and tears are both responses to frustration and exhaustion. I myself prefer to laugh, since there is less cleaning up to do afterward.* —Kurt Vonnegut[7]

Today's families are indeed living in tenuous times within a culture that is still in the process of figuring out how digitally enhanced life works. This new culture has swept in so quickly and spread so pervasively that it often feels like some big scary menace.

Do not be discouraged! We described today's parents in an earlier chapter as trailblazers. As Christian parents, we are well suited for this task. We know there is always hope for the future. We trust that God is working through us, at our best or worst, in mysterious and powerful ways. There may be tears along the path, but our kids are just as likely to remember a lot of great times laughing at and about digital media with us. Look for ways to laugh together at these new challenges as an expression of your faithfulness and resilience in the face of it all.

In fact, since we often chuckled at parents' brilliant insights and humorous solutions to their digital media dilemmas, we end this book with a handful of our favorite quotes from parents. May they remind you that as your family blazes its own technology trail, you are not alone.

"Our daughter complains that we know everything she's doing online, and we're just like, 'Bingo. Score one for the home team.'"

—NOAH, DAD OF ONE

"If our kids spend time messing around online, they have to do chores to earn more time so they can get their online homework done. I've gotten my toilet cleaned a lot. That's my go-to chore. I try to use my own laziness to my advantage. It's great."

—BECKY, MOM OF TWO

"I actually cut the cord once. We were arguing about them watching TV. I turned it off; they turned it back on. I unplugged it; they plugged it back in. So I got my scissors, walked in very casually, pulled the plug from the wall, and cut the end of it off. The kids were flabbergasted."

—APRIL, MOM OF FOUR

"One of our kids asked us if they could un-friend their grandmother on Facebook because she comments so much on everything. I told them no. But honestly … I was sort of wondering the same thing!"

—JILL, MOM OF FOUR

"My daughter came running in one day and said, 'Dad, did you know Kevin is dating someone? He just posted it online.' And I said, 'Yeah, I knew.' And she was like, 'How did you know?' I said, 'Kevin cleaned out his car and washed it last weekend. Guys don't do that unless they have a date.' I didn't need social media to figure that one out."

—JIM, DAD OF TWO

"My husband loves playing Minecraft, which is a building game, with our boys. I caught him playing it once in the middle of the night. He was downstairs building his little village or whatever, trying to beat the boys! I took away his screen time privileges the next day, and the boys burned down his village. Serves him right."

—SUSAN, MOM OF THREE

"The assistant principal at their school sent this email with a list of all the students who were at risk of flunking, with reasons why for each one. It was supposed to go to the teachers, but he sent it to every parent at the school. Whoops! Looks like the kids aren't the only ones who screw up."

—TODD, DAD OF THREE

# DISCUSSION QUESTIONS

 1 Think about a few interactions you've had with your kids involving digital media; were you in architect, mentor, or companion mode? Are there any times you responded in one mode but wish, in hindsight, that you had approached it differently?

2 Do you feel more at ease about any of the anxieties you may have had prior to reading this book? Have your primary concerns or goals about digital media shifted at all?

3 What did you think of the suggestion to partner with your kids to help you change how you use digital media?

4   How do you feel about working more with other parents to help you navigate digital media? Are there any parents you've met through school, church, or other activities that might be good to connect with online or even have coffee with?

5   What's the next step with your family digital covenant or vision statement? Do you need to write it down, post it in your home, or talk through some of these issues around the dinner table? Decide what "covenant" looks like in your family and what you will do to help one another live out the commitments you agree to keep.

# ··· APPENDIX ············

## 10 THINGS EVERY PARENT SHOULD KNOW ABOUT GAMING

1.  Researchers have helpfully identified three reasons people play digital games: **to kill time, to hang out, and for recreation.**[1]

    ***Killing time*** refers to quick games kids play when they have a few minutes to spare between activities. Using a handheld game or puzzle to fill moments like this is certainly nothing new. App games have replaced distractions like the marbles or Rubik's Cubes of yesteryear.

    ***Hanging out*** is probably what most of us envision as the "typical" teen mode of gaming—playing games with friends and family as a way to relax and escape the stresses of everyday life.

    ***Recreational gaming*** refers to when someone specifically wants to play a game—with or without others. The game is no longer just filling the void of "nothing better to do."

    These categories offer helpful distinctions; if a person or group is looking for something to do and chooses to play video games, it is *hanging out*. If they specifically want to make time for playing video games, it is *recreational*. This does not make recreational gaming inherently bad, it just means this type of play has become a more intentional hobby. And **hobbies become an important part of a young person's identity.**

2. Gaming has become pervasive enough that it brings some measure of the same social benefits young people find from other hobbies: practicing to master certain skills, feelings of achievement outside of the classroom, and respect from peers.

   A number of studies have also found that gaming has potential to be a healthy, positive recreational activity. Games have been found to improve perceptual skills, visual attention, and spatial skills, and they can be powerful learning tools.[2]

   **Contrary to how we often perceive gaming, it is *not* necessarily an inferior alternative to other activities like art, music, drama, or sports.** Gaming has become an important and [mostly] healthy part of teen culture that can equip young people in distinct ways for future careers in fields like engineering, architecture, and information/technology.

3. Recent data suggests that teens in the US spend an average of one hour and thirteen minutes playing video games, three to four days per week (roughly four or five hours total per week).[3] If your kids are playing much more than this and arguing that "everyone" gets to play more, you can actually defend yourself with data.

4. The amount of time spent gaming peaks between the ages of eight and thirteen and then tapers off for many young people. This doesn't mean parents should cut kids off after their fourteenth birthday, but **it may alleviate some of your concern to know that kids' interest is likely to wane as they get older.**

5. Gaming might be a problem when it becomes disruptive to other responsibilities such as homework and chores. If a young person begins skipping these other duties, it could be a sign that their gaming is becoming unhealthy.

**If kids are playing too often or for too long, but still managing to get their responsibilities taken care of, they may just need other recreational options.** Talk with your kids about their interests, and then ask other parents or church leaders for some suggestions.

6.  Taking breaks while playing is extremely important. Gamers can fall into a "flow" state comparable to gambling when they play for long periods of time. Some games have been designed to break this flow with timed levels and narrative sequences; others cater to it by offering endless, continuous action.

    Extended gaming sessions of an hour or more should only be allowed if short breaks are taken frequently throughout. **The way television shows are broken up might be a good rule: brief interruptions every fifteen minutes, a short break every thirty minutes, and a longer break after an hour.**

7.  There are now more adult gamers than ever before, which means **there are more games made specifically for an adult audience.** Keep track of the games your kids are playing to make sure the content is appropriate, just like you would for movies or music. We encourage you to check out the Entertainment Software Rating Board (ESRB) website: www. esrb.org. This organization is responsible for assigning video game ratings, and they offer a lot of great resources for parents.

8.  Most video game consoles and devices have built-in features that allow parents to limit how long their children can play, restrict accessing the Internet through the system, and in some cases even block games above a certain content rating (e.g., "T for Teen" or "M for Mature"). In addition to info on game ratings, the ESRB website can help you set these up.

9. A common trick young people pull is to ask extended family members and friends to give them games with higher ratings than appropriate for birthdays or as Christmas presents. **If your kids have a generous grandmother or unassuming uncle from whom they typically receive gifts, make sure these folks know what your standards are and how to check ratings.**

10. Several parents told us that their kids (sons in particular) would get extremely angry while playing certain games. **While games can be a good cathartic outlet for adolescents, and part of what makes any game fun is yelling and getting excited when the action picks up, make sure this doesn't get out of hand.** Encourage kids to stop playing games that elicit intense anger and instead opt for others that are equally as fun and challenging. Some parents have noticed that games in which players are first-person shooters are especially prone to producing excessive anger, so keep that in mind as you're making gaming decisions as a family.

    One mom told us that she took a particular game away because of the way it stirred up rage in her son, but she also bought him a replacement game so he wouldn't feel punished. "I just didn't like the game, and when we talked about it he kind of realized, 'Wow, it is stupid to get so mad about a game.' So I let him pick out a new one that was fun but a little more mellow."

# ENDNOTES

## LOGIN [PREFACE]

1. This phrase is attributed to the Prayer of St. Francis and is also popularly used in modern discussion as one of Stephen R. Covey's *The 7 Habits of Highly Effective People* (1989).

2. Vern L. Bengtson, Norella M. Putney, and Susan Harris, *Families and Faith* (New York: Oxford University Press, 2013). This finding has been confirmed by multiple studies across a variety of faith traditions over the past three decades. See stickyfaith. org for more resources to help nurture lifelong faith.

3. Statistics compiled from Pew Research Center, "Teens, Social Media & Technology Overview 2015," April 9, 2015: http:// www.pewinternet.org/2015/04/09/teens-social-media-technology-2015/ and Pew Research Center, "Teens, Technology and Friendships," August 6, 2015: http://www.pewinternet. org/2015/08/06/teens-technology-and-friendships.

## CHAPTER 1

1. For the sake of privacy, all names and identifying information have been changed throughout the book.

2. Alan Kay, "Distracting Ourselves to Death" (plenary address presented at the annual meeting of the Media Ecology Association, St. Louis, MO, June 20, 2009).

3. Sonia Livingstone, *Children and the Internet* (Malden, MA: Polity Press, 2009), 10-32.

4. Raymond Williams, *Keywords: A Vocabulary of Culture and Society* (New York: Oxford University Press, 2014), 203.

5. You might notice that we use "media" (the plural for "medium") as a singular in this book. We know it's technically incorrect. Typical to common use, we found that a lot of parents we interviewed used it as singular, and we opted to do the same.

6. See Paul Jones and David Holmes, *Key Concepts in Media and Communications* (London: Sage Publications, 2011), 62-65.

7. Walter Isaacson traces the evolution of each of these separate inventions and how they were integrated into a singular digital media in his 2014 book, *The Innovators: How a Group of Hackers, Geniuses, and Geeks Created the Digital Revolution* (Simon and Shuster).

8. John Durham Peters, *The Marvelous Clouds: Toward a Philosophy of Elemental Media* (Chicago: University of Chicago Press, 2015).

9. Media scholars use this metaphor, and the term "mediatization," to describe the paradigm shift from analog to digital media. See: Kurt Lundby, ed. *Mediatization: Concept, Changes, Consequences* (New York: Peter Lang, 2009); L.A. Lievrouw, "New Media, Mediation, and Communication Study 1," *Information, Communication & Society* 12 (3), 303-325; Andreas Hepp and Franz Krotz, eds. *Mediatized Worlds: Culture and Society in a Media Age,* (New York: Palgrave Macmillan, 2014), 72-88.

10. Sonia Livingstone, Lucyna Kirwil, Cristina Ponte, and Elisabeth Staksrud, "In their own words: What bothers children online?" *European Journal of Communication* 29 (3), 271-288.

11. We do know that the ways in which people use digital media vary according to their socioeconomic status and geographic location. This means that the exact same study might find radically different things when conducted in the UK versus the US, South America, etc.

12. Lynn Schofield Clark, "Parental mediation theory for the digital age," *Communication Theory* 21 (4), 323-343.

13. Annette Markham and Nancy K. Baym, eds., *Internet Inquiry: Conversations About Method* (Thousand Oaks, CA: Sage, 2008).

14. In Alan Deutschman's 2008 book, *Change or Die: Could You Change When Change Matters Most* (Harper Collins), he describes the three keys to change as: relate, repeat, and reframe. We need new hope, new skills, and new thinking in order to enact meaningful, lasting change. The other resources we reviewed on this topic typically focused on the new skills component without new hope or new thinking to bolster them.

15. Christian Smith and Melissa Lundquist Denton, *Soul Searching* (New York: Oxford University Press, 2005), 57. The importance of parental example is confirmed in a number of studies, including Pam E. King and Ross A. Mueller, "Parental Influence on Adolescent Religiousness: Exploring the Roles of Spiritual Modeling and Social Capital," *Marriage and Family: A Christian Journal* 6, no. 3 (2003): 401-13.

16. Lynn Schofield Clark, *The Parent App: Understanding Families in the Digital Age* (Oxford University Press, 2013), 157-159.

## *CHAPTER 2*

1.  See: Walter Isaacson, *The Innovators: How a Group of Inventors, Hackers, Geniuses and Geeks Created the Digital Revolution* (New York: Simon and Schuster, 2014); and Michael A. Hiltzik, *Dealers of Lightning: Xerox PARC and the Dawn of the Computer Age* (New York: HarperCollins, 1999).

2. John Palfrey and Uls Gasser, *Born Digital: Understanding the First Generation of Digital Natives* (Philadelphia: Basic Books, 2010).

3. George Gerbner, Larry Gross, Michael Morgan, and Nanoy Signorielli, "Living with Television: The Dynamics of the Cultivation Process," in *Perspectives on Media Effects* (Hillsdale, NJ: Erlbaum, 1986), 17-40.

4.  Marie Winn, "The plug-in generation," *Change: The Magazine of Higher Learning*, May-June 1985, 14-20.

5.  Jennings Bryant and Mary Beth Oliver, eds., *Media Effects: Advances in Theory and Research* (New York: Routledge, 2008).

6.  Richard Jackson Harris and Fred W. Sanborn, *A Cognitive Psychology of Mass Communication* (New York: Routledge, 2013), 31-34.

7.  Charles Babbage, *Passages from the Life of a Philosopher* (Cambridge: Cambridge University Press, 2011). Babbage is credited with originating the concept of a programmable computer.

8.  See Rosalind Wiseman, *Queen Bees and Wannabes: Helping Your Daughter Survive Cliques, Gossip, Boyfriends, and the New Realities of Girl World* (New York: Three Rivers Press, 2009).

9.  Nancy K. Baym, *Personal Connections in the Digital Age* (Malden, MA: Polity Press, 2010), 59-71.

10. Edmund Carpenter, *Oh, What a Blow That Phantom Gave Me!* (New York: Bantam Books, 1974), 34.

11. danah boyd, *It's Complicated: The Social Lives of Networked Teens* (New Haven, CT: Yale University Press, 2014). Note that boyd prefers her name without capital letters.

# CHAPTER 3

1.  Nick Couldry, *Media Rituals: A Critical Approach* (New York: Routledge, 2003). Also Paul Jones and David Holmes, *Key Concepts in Media and Communications* (London: Sage Publications, 2011), 193 – 197.

2.  See Mizuko Itō et al., *Hanging Out, Messing Around, and Geeking Out: Kids Living and Learning With New Media* (Cambridge, MA: MIT Press, 2010).

3. Michelle M. Garrison, Kimberly Liekweg, and Dimitri A. Christakis, "Media use and child sleep: the impact of content, timing, and environment," *Pediatrics* 128 (1), 29-35; Anne-Marie Chang, Daniel Aeschbach, Jeanne F. Duffy, and Charles A. Czeisler, "Evening use of light-emitting eReaders negatively affects sleep, circadian timing, and next-morning alertness," *Proceedings of the National Academy of Sciences*, 112 (January 27, 2015): 1232-1237.

4. However, be advised that for teens these types of restrictions often become like the old "Going on a Bear Hunt" song: Can't go over it, can't go under it, can't go around it, got to go through it! If they really want to, they'll try any which way until they figure out how to get through your barrier. Carl happened to work in I.T. and warned us, "Don't try to outsmart teens with this stuff unless you're *really good.*" Or at least don't be surprised *when they beat your game.*

## CHAPTER 4

1. Janis Wolak, Kimberly Mitchell, and David Finkelhor, "Unwanted and wanted exposure to online pornography in a national sample of youth Internet users," *Pediatrics* 119 (2), 247-257.

2. Sonia Livingstone, *Children and the Internet,* (Malden, MA: Polity Press, 2009), 151-180.

3. Lynn Schofield Clark, *The Parent App: Understanding Families in the Digital Age* (New York: Oxford University Press, 2014), 49-71.

4. boyd, *It's Complicated: The Social Lives of Networked Teens*, 100-127.

5. Ibid., 127

6. Art Bamford, "Exclusive Interview with danah boyd: What you wish you knew about teens and digital media," Fuller Youth

Institute, https://fulleryouthinstitute.org/articles/viamedia-danahboyd.

7.  See: Erica Weintraub Austin, Stacey J.T. Hust, and Michelle E. Kistler, "Powerful Media Tools: Arming Parents with Strategies to Affect Children's Interactions with Commercial Interests," in *Parents and Children Communicating with Society: Managing Relationships Outside of Home,* ed. Thomas J. Socha and Glen H. Stamp (New York: Routledge, 2009), 215-240; and Amy I. Nathanson, "Mediation of children's television viewing: Working toward conceptual clarity and common understanding," in *Communication Yearbook, Vol. 25,* William B. Gudykunst, ed., (Mahwah, NJ: Lawrence Erlbaum, 2001), 115-151.

8.  It is important to note that this kind of study proves correlation, which is different from causation. We cannot prove that conversations are the causative factor, but they are correlated with negative attitudes about porn and lower porn viewing. Eric E. Rasmussen, Rebecca R. Ortiz, and Shawna R. White, "Emerging Adults' Responses to Active Mediation of Pornography During Adolescence," *Journal of Children and Media* (January 13, 2015), 1-17.

9.  Livingstone, *Children and the Internet,* 202-238.

10. You may wonder: Why don't they just do this? It seems like a no-brainer! These kinds of restrictions raise very complex First Amendment and intellectual property related issues. The current approach is to wait and see how things play out rather than immediately create legislation that will end up being challenged in courts for decades.

11. Andy Stanley in conversation with Billy Phoenix, *Transit Sex Series* produced by North Point Ministries, 2015. http://transitstudents.org/transit-sex-series-parent-page/

12. Donald D. Strassberg, Ryan K. McKinnon, Michael A. Sustaíta, and Jordan Rullo, "Sexting by high school students: An exploratory and descriptive study," *Archives of Sexual Behavior* 42 (1): 15-21.

13. Marshall Smith, "Youth viewing sexually explicit material online: Addressing the elephant on the screen," *Sexuality Research and Social Policy* 10, no. 1 (2013): 62-75.

14. Clark, *The Parent App,* 157-159.

15. We recommend that parents do not rely solely on celebrity/magazine endorsements, customer reviews, or the popularity rankings of these tools. Companies use these as ways to market their products and can manipulate what looks like user feedback more than we assume.

## CHAPTER 5

1. User comment posted anonymously on the Yik Yak app in Pasadena, CA on April 24, 2014.

2. This description is taken from Yik Yak's page in Apple's App Store. The issues we experienced locally with this app were partly because there are several colleges and universities in the area. The mix of high school students interacting anonymously with college students was not one parents and schools were too keen on. This app is clearly labeled as appropriate for ages 17+ in Apple's App Store.

3. Louis "C.K." Székely, appearance on *Late Night with Conan O'Brien* (NBC), September 17, 2009.

4. John Suler, "The online disinhibition effect," *CyberPsychology & Behavior* 7 (June 2004): 321-326.

5. See Ciaran McMahon and Mary Aiken, "Privacy as identity territoriality: Re-conceptualising behaviour in cyberspace," available at SSRN 2390934 (February 4, 2014).

6. Walter J. Ong, *Orality and Literacy: The Technologizing of the Word* (New York: Routledge, 2012). See also: Jonathan Sterne, "The theology of sound: A critique of orality," *Canadian Journal*

*of Communication*, 36 (2). Sterne helpfully separates the wheat from chaff with regards to how Ong's work has been used and applied by media scholars since it was originally published.

7.  Rosalind Wiseman, *Masterminds and Wingmen: Helping Our Boys Cope with Schoolyard Power, Locker-Room Tests, Girlfriends, and the New Rules of Boy World* (New York: Harmony, 2014), 155.

8.  Michelle F. Wright, "Predictors of anonymous cyber aggression: The role of adolescents' beliefs about anonymity, aggression, and the permanency of digital content," *Cyberpsychology, Behavior, and Social Networking* 17 (7), 431-438.

9.  Bertrand Russell, *On Education* (New York: Routledge, 2014), 50.

10. Jaron Lanier, "Digital Maoism: The hazards of the new online collectivism," *The Edge*, May 29, 2006, 183.

# CHAPTER 6

1.  John Lennon, "Beautiful Boy (Darling Boy)," *Double Fantasy* (New York: Geffen Records, 1980).

2.  Clark, *The Parent App*, 158.

3.  Clark, *The Parent App*, 213. See also Hara Estroff Marano, *A Nation of Wimps: The High Cost of Invasive Parenting* (New York: Broadway Books, 2008).

4.  Ibid.

5.  danah boyd is very critical of addiction language with regard to how young people use media. Addictive patterns of behavior are also more prevalent among adolescents because of their cognitive development at this stage—they are more emotional, less thoughtful, and more sensitive to rewards. See Michael Grabowski, ed., *Neuroscience and Media: New Understandings and Representations* (New York: Routledge, 2014).

6. danah boyd, interview with Fuller Youth Institute, "Work with youth ... that is the core of authenticity for them." See Art Bamford, "Exclusive interview with danah boyd: What you wish you knew about teens and digital media," https://fulleryouthinstitute.org/articles/viamedia-danahboyd.

7. Kurt Vonnegut, "Hypocrites You Always Have With You," *The Nation* 230 (15): 469.

## *APPENDIX*

1. Mizuko Itō et al., *Hanging Out, Messing Around, and Geeking Out: Kids Living and Learning With New Media.*

2. Lavinia McLean and Mark Griffiths, "The psychological effects of videogames on young people," *Aloma* 31 (1): 19-133. See also Richard De Lisi and Jennifer L. Wolford, "Improving children's mental rotation accuracy with computer game playing," *Journal of Genetic Psychology* 163 (3): 272-282.; Jing Feng, Ian Spence, and Jay Pratt, "Playing an action video game reduces gender differences in spatial cognition," *Psychological Science* 18 (10): 850-855; C. Shawn Green and Daphne Bavelier, "Action video games modify visual selective attention," *Nature* 423 (May 29, 2003): 534- 537; C. Shawn Green and Daphne Bavelier, "Enumeration versus multiple object tracking: The case of action video game players," *Cognition* 101 (August 2006): 217-245.

3. "Generation M[2:] Media in the Lives of 8-to 18-Year-Olds. A Kaiser Family Foundation Study," a survey by *The Kaiser Family Foundation,* 2010, available at: http://kff.org.